To M
what
have had . . . .
lord continue to lead you

VITAL
SIGNS

to greater abundance and
joy!

DISCOVERING THE KEYS TO
ABUNDANT CHRISTIAN LIVING

Much Love —
David

DAVID SWANSON

 Conversant Media Group

Published by Conversant Media Group, Huntington Beach, CA. www.ConversantMediaGroup.com

Published in association with the literary agency of Wolgemuth & Associates, Inc.

FIRST EDITION

Cover design and layout by Rafael and Megan Polendo (rpjrdesign.com)
Cover images © Rosemary Calvert / Getty Images

Library of Congress Cataloging-in-Publication Data is available upon request.

ISBN 978-0-9819515-3-9

Printed in the United States of America.

TABLE OF CONTENTS

For Leigh
You are the joy in my journey

And for John David, Alex and Kaylee
My precious children who daily enrich my life and bring me
the abundance of God's blessings

ACKNOWLEDGMENTS

This book has been percolating inside of me for a number of years, and I am grateful for the opportunity to finally get it down on paper and into God's hands for His use and glory. It grew from my repeated observations of people who claimed the name of Christ, but were the exact opposite of the word "abundance." They seemed to be slogging through life with no joy, and discordant nature of their lives was troubling to me.

The more I read and observed, and the more I served in the day to day role of being a pastor, the more God revealed some core issues to me. Make no mistake, these core issues were revealed by God as shortcomings *in my own life*. I am far from the model disciple, but I do believe that God wants us to know the abundance He promised. Abundance does not mean circumstantial ease or comfort, either. Abundance is completely held in the love and grace of God present in our lives.

I want to thank my wife, Leigh, and my children, John David, Alex and Kaylee. Writing this book has taken a lot of hours, but they have patiently, and sometimes humorously, walked along with me. I am also grateful for my dear friend Robert Wolgemuth. Robert was the chair of the search committee that called me to First Presbyterian Church six years ago, and he has been a trusted brother ever since. His wisdom in the writing and publishing world has been invaluable in this process. Andrew Wolgemuth has also been a huge help in keeping me on track.

I am blessed with one of the finest Executive Assistants that God has ever placed on earth. Paula Lindrum takes care of me in every conceivable way, and does so with not only grace, but excellence. She has the burden of putting up with me, for which she is compensated far too little. I am also grateful to the men in my small group who were with me when this vision started—Robb, Mark, Scott, Robert and Justin. Your steadfast love and support of me along this journey has been one of God's great blessings.

Finally, I am grateful to the congregations that I have served. The dear saints at Signal Mountain Presbyterian

Church who loved me and nurtured me in my early days in ministry, not to mention helping me raise my children; the gracious people of Covenant Presbyterian Church in Ft. Myers who put up with my mistakes and faithfully allowed ministry to flourish; and the faithful, loving people of First Presbyterian Church in Orlando who love me and my family in such supportive and renewing ways that I cannot imagine a better place to serve the Lord.

INTRODUCTION

*"I have come that they may have life and have it
to the full"*

As I approach my 20th year of ordained ministry, I sometimes chuckle at the number of times I hear myself, or a colleague, say, "they didn't teach me that in seminary." Don't get me wrong, I loved my seminary education. However, nothing can possibly prepare a person for what ministry is like outside the classroom. There were no classes offered for "what to do when the groom throws up during the wedding" or "what to do when hurricanes devastate your community" or "what to do when you accidentally throw the communion bread on the floor." These are things you have to learn as you go, and my goodness, I have learned a lot.

In God's sovereign plan, He has taken me to three very unique and different churches, but each one presented a common theme: restoration. In each one, I had to prayerfully consider: how do I lead in such a way that this church or ministry can experience a spiritual revitalization? How can I lead them such that they will know the "abundant living" promised by Jesus in John 10:10?

To be sure, I learned as much, if not more, from my mistakes as I did my successes, but in either case, I was learning. God was revealing Himself to me and to those that I served. As He did, a common question emerged: If people profess faith in Jesus, yet do not live out of His joy or abundance, then where is the disconnect? It seemed that over and over again, I would encounter people who professed deep faith in God, but whose lives did not reflect the promised abundance. Not only did I see it in them, but I found it to be true in my own life.

Perhaps my biggest mistake in ministry was trying to will transformation in people's lives. At one point, I was so consumed by my own efforts and creative ideas to revitalize a church that I completely omitted God from the process. I was going to do it by the sheer force of my determination and work ethic. Right. Try that. See how it works for you. I was trying to lead people towards abundant living, but I didn't know it myself. Guess what? I didn't lead them very far or very well.

Psalm 30 became a constant refrain for me as I found my heart crying out "of the depths." I had to address certain habits and ways of thinking in my own life before I was going to lead effectively towards vitality in Christ. From that posture of searching, the contents of this book began to emerge. The lessons became the foundation for a sermon series that I initially preached in Ft. Myers. With revision and further growth, I preached it again at First Presbyterian, Orlando, shortly after my arrival in 2004. In both churches, God has been so faithful to do what I could never do on my own: revitalize and heal people and communities.

Because of seeing God's work in such palpable ways, I could not get the idea or question out of my mind. The Holy Spirit kept pushing me to write it down and get it out. Four years ago, I started that process, and—finally—it has come to fruition. For that, I am grateful, but let me also say there is no "magic pill" for abundant living. What I have learned and what I try to share in these pages is that the abundance and joy of our life in Christ is cultivated through the simplicity of basic spiritual discipline.

Too often, I think we depend on a new program, a new study, or a new mountaintop experience to get us going. The reality is that we need to invest more in the daily walk of discipleship instead of constantly searching for the next spiritual fix. Yes, those things can help, but an abundant Christian life is one carved out over years of faithfully engaging in the basics—the solid food of God's Word, the power of worship, the blessing of community, the joy of giving, the sense of purpose derived from mission. These are some of the elements through which God pours out His life in us.

I pray that as you read, you will find a deep hunger to know more of these things—and more of the presence of God—in your life. It is not something I have mastered by any means, but it is a journey I humbly share with you.

Part One

IN SEARCH OF AN ABUNDANT CHRISTIAN LIFE

1

"People will be lovers of themselves, lovers of money, boastful, proud, abusive, disobedient to their parents, ungrateful, unholy, without love, unforgiving, slanderous, without self-control, brutal, not lovers of the good, treacherous, rash, conceited, lovers of pleasure rather than lovers of God—having a form of godliness but denying its power..."

2 TIMOTHY 3:2-5

Because I had been asked to teach a workshop at a national oncology conference, my wife and I found ourselves at a beautiful beach resort in south Florida in the spring of 2005. The event drew doctors and researchers from all over the world eager to learn from the best in their fields; of course, the white sandy beaches, glorious pool, spacious rooms, and great restaurants didn't hurt either. It was heaven for a pastor and his wife who don't get out much! Even better—it was free! As you can imagine, we were very excited as we arrived for our four-day, mini-vacation.

When we pulled up to the hotel, the valet took our car and a hostess inquired as to whether or not we were attending the conference. I said we were and introduced myself, to which she enthusiastically replied, "Dr. Swanson, we're so happy you're here! I hope you'll enjoy the many lectures and seminars we've arranged for you."

Now, just so you know, I am a doctor, but my doctorate is in theology, not medicine. Trust me, as my seminary supervisor (or my wife) could testify, you don't want me in an operating room. However, not wanting to be impolite, I shrugged it off and followed her to the registration desk.

At registration, a young lady found our file, pulled out our registration forms, and handed us our name tags. My wife's tag said, "Leigh Swanson—Conference Presenter," but for some reason, my name tag said "David Swanson, MD—Conference Presenter."

It was an honest mistake, especially considering we were attending a conference full of medical doctors. I can understand a little Greek, but I wouldn't stand a chance attempting to decipher a medical chart. Naturally, I started to correct the mistake, but then a little voice in my head said, "Wait a second—this could be fun—go with it!"

So with a playful swagger, I draped the name badge around my neck proclaiming to the world, "David Swanson, MD." My mother would have been so proud.

We lingered in the lobby for a few minutes, chatting casually with other doctors and their spouses. No one asked any technical questions. No one assumed I was a phony, but it wasn't long until I met the fate I deserved. Leigh and I decided to go up to our room to get ready for dinner, so we walked across the lobby to the bank of elevators. The doors opened and we stepped in, but just as the doors were closing, another man joined us.

At large medical conferences, in addition to the doctors you would expect, a variety of sales representatives are also in attendance. They have a captive audience for promoting all the latest medical gadgets and they want to sell, sell, sell! We were not immune. Ten seconds into our ride up, it was clear our elevator companion had an agenda.

He took one look at my badge and stuck out his hand. "Dr. Swanson, I'm Joe Jones. I think I called on you in Oregon. How's your practice going?" Once again, my mischievous nature got the best of me, and I decided to see how long I could fake my new identity.

"I think you have the wrong guy, Joe," I said. "I've never practiced in Oregon."

"Oh, I'm sorry. Where is your practice located?"

"Just recently set up shop in Orlando," I replied, gathering all the bravado I could muster. As I did, my wife, Leigh, flashed me one of those "what-do-you-think-you're-doing?" glares. I smiled at her and continued: "Yeah, we love it there and my practice is really growing."

Now he was curious. "That's great," he said. "Have you taken advantage of the blah, blah, blah protocol? What do you consider the catalyst of your growth?"

No question, I was in trouble. My mind was racing. The words he was using sounded vaguely like surgical instruments, so I guessed.

"No," I said, "I'm not a surgeon. I specialize in finding signs of internal growth."

"Really?" Joe countered. "So, your practice is in,…?"

I hesitated briefly, searching for an answer that might get me out of this mess.

"Ummmm,…well, once I find signs of growth, I work with the patient towards full restoration. It's a very holistic approach."

Joe's face scrunched up with a puzzled-look. I could tell that he was about to continue his questioning. But thankfully, the doors opened on his floor and he got off. "Sounds interesting," Joe said as he stepped out. "Perhaps I can hear more about it sometime…."

"Love to," I said, as the doors closed, my voice trailing off, hoping never to see him again. Leigh was not pleased, and while it may have not been my finest moment, I was pretty impressed with myself for surviving 18 floors!

For the remainder of the conference, I was more well-behaved (much to my wife's delight) and found many of the presentations riveting. There was one break-out room devoted to nothing but video about disease progression, groundbreaking techniques for treatment, new medications, and associated statistical data. The longer I lingered, the more overwhelmed I felt by the sheer volume of data. I knew that each figure was more than a number; it was a life. A life that hurt and struggled and worried—a life inextricably bound to friends and family and children. A life that was precious.

Sure, I knew plenty of people with cancer, but I had no idea how pervasive it was. Standing in that room, surrounded by the harsh reality of suffering and disease, I was moved by a sense of urgency; a sense of urgency that I'm sure motivated the "real" doctors at the conference as well. It didn't seem quite so fun anymore. It had become grave and real and disturbing.

A Different Kind of Illness

If someone from the American Cancer Society had come up to me at that moment asking for a donation, I would have opened my checkbook and poured out its contents. I was

motivated. I was moved. I wanted to do something—anything—to help. However, that was not the end of my experience at the conference nor the end of the feelings that
had been stirred up in me. My purpose in being there in the
first place was to lead a seminar on the relationship between
spirituality and healing. Because of the wide variety of religious persuasions represented at the conference, I had been
asked to not be overtly Christian in my presentation. Even
so, I was very clear about who I was and what I believed.

As so often happens, once I identified myself as a pastor,
people—doctors in this case—approached me between ses-
sions, after meals, and even at the pool. They would begin with
typical chit-chat, but sure enough, eventually, they arrived
at the real point of their curiosity; much like their patients,
they too, were sick and in need of healing. However, cancer
was not the problem. Their wounds came in many different
forms. Among the members of this elite group of doctors, I
found many who were hurting, living spiritually unhealthy
lives. Despite all the external signs of success, internally, they
yearned for something to make them well, and they were asking me how to find it. Some were involved in extra-marital
affairs. Some were struggling with how to cope with dying
patients. Some wanted to know how to answer the difficult
questions they were being asked about morality and eternity.

Oddly, there was no sign of these painful revelations during the conference's evening events. Tuxedoed, beautifully-
adorned, lavishly-jeweled people sipped on bubbly drinks
and ate caviar while doing a fabulous job of pretending that
all was right with the world. The appearances of health and
vitality were all around us, but inside, I knew there were
many who were sick. And dying.

Some of these doctors were depressed. Some were guilt-
ridden by the lack of time with their families. Some were
struggling with alcoholism and/or drug abuse. Some were
just desperate for hope, to find some meaning to their work
and their lives.

After four days of listening, teaching and watching, Leigh
and I packed our bags and started our journey home. In a
short format like the one we had been in, it is hard to do much
to help people other than listen, because most of the time, you
never see them again. Everyone goes back to living their every
day lives. As a pastor, that can be very frustrating, and I felt a

sense of guilt at not having been able to do more. As we drove back to Orlando, we were overwhelmed by the same feelings we had had that first day while standing in the display room. Initially, I was overwhelmed by the reality of physical illness and cancer. By the end, I was overwhelmed by the pervasive nature of spiritually sick hearts—hearts yearning to be healed. It was painful, and yet I was also moved. I wanted to do something.

After a decade and a half of ministry, I was motivated like never before. Yes, there are many people who are sick, but cancer is only one problem. There are many physical ailments that threaten us, but what I had become painfully aware of was far greater than just a physical illness. It was a spiritual illness. It was a heart problem, and without correction, a problem with negative eternal consequences.

After this realization, I was naturally focused on others. I had found a problem with all the "other" people; a problem that conveniently did not involve me. But God soon corrected that. He led me to a rather painful discovery: *the patient was me.* No matter how much I fought it, no matter how much I didn't want to acknowledge it, the truth of the matter was that I was the one who was sick. I kept trying to tell God why that wasn't right, but He kept bringing me back to the undeniable fact that I needed healing.

In the wake of the conference, I would rise each morning to seek God's direction for the writing of this book. For a period of days I made no progress because He kept bringing the conversation back to me. Like any preacher, I felt I was supposed to be the one with the answers—the one equipped to tell others what to do—but suddenly I realized God had much more to say to me in this process.

During this time, a Christian band, Switchfoot, had a popular song on the radio with a chorus that kept hammering my soul: "This is your life—are you who you want to be?" I continued to ask myself that question. God kept pushing me: How have you grown? What have you done to make your relationship with me more vital? How have you become more Christ-like in the past five years? Paul came bellowing at me from Ephesians 5:1 with the admonition to, "live a life of love, just as Christ loved us." I had to ask myself, "Am I more loving, more Christ-like? In what ways am growing into a healthier child of God?"

Unfortunately, while the questions multiplied, the answers did not. What I found to be true in my own life is what I believe haunts many of us: we are surviving, but we are not *growing*. We are not thriving. We move from one crisis to the next—one challenge to the next—with the intent of "getting through it" but not growing in it. We think that, because of the urgent things that crowd around us, we have no time for growth, or that we will simply grow by osmosis. We have no intent—no desire. We think we have enough faith to go on, so we settle for mediocrity, and in the process, we flatline. Someone grab the paddles! We are void of *any* spiritual vital signs. We're breathing, but the heartbeat is faint.

Let me try to explain what I've learned about living in "survivor mode." You may survive, but each survival comes at a price; it exacts a toll such that, at some point, you are depleted. Your energy—your vitality—is lost. You don't thrive, you just survive. It's not a healthy way to live.

In my life, I've survived a long-distance move with my family into a broken church. I've survived a painful rebuilding process when there was scarcely little nurturing to be found and an attempt by some congregants to fire me. I've survived two collapsed lungs and the surgeries that followed. I've survived another move to another wounded congregation and my own misguided attempt to *will* a healing to take place. Did I survive these things? Yes. Was I thriving? No. Why not? I had assumed that my faith was enough to see me through, and while it was, I had done nothing to nurture that faith such that my life in Christ remained healthy and vital. I was surviving, but I was not growing.

That realization was the real turning point for me. No matter who you are or what you do, you cannot neglect your spiritual health. We all need a proper spiritual diet. We need to avoid the wrong influences. We need the living water of community. We need the solid food of worship and God's Word. We need the nourishment that comes through serving.

As a little boy, my favorite show was the Lone Ranger. I used to love how he would come out of nowhere to save the day, then ride off into the sunset without a care in the world. For a long time, I wanted to be him. Strong. Independent. Free. In fact, for a long time, I *was* him. However, the lesson in my life—and in this book—is that the "Lone Ranger Christian" does not survive. We need to grow, and we grow by

being surrounded by and connected to Christ and to others.
Thus, as you will see from these pages, I think the Church is
very important. I don't think we can disconnect our spiritual
health from the God-given community in which He intends
for us to find it. Paul's words to Timothy at the beginning of
this chapter sum up the realities of our world very well. Living farther and farther apart from God, our culture is exhibit-
ing the advancing signs of illness and disease. However, it is
not just *them*, it is us—and we'd better start figuring out how
to get better.

Trying to Get Well

So, how do we do that? We live in a world where people are
more conscious than ever of what makes them healthy, what
might help stem the tide of illness. Television, the internet
and newspapers are filled with stories about the latest tools,
techniques and medications to improve our physical and
emotional health. We need to eat right, exercise, meditate and
stretch. We need to slim down, shape up, chill out and breathe
in. We need to channel our anger, make peace with our fear,
and nurture our inner-child. We need to sleep more, work
less, find ourselves, and lose our inhibitions. Of course, even
with access to more information than we could ever consume,
the magic bullet remains a moving target.

Not long ago, the *New York Times* reported, "Low Fat Diet
Does Not Cut Health Risks, Study Shows." When I saw the
headline, I laughed out loud. For years and years, people
who wanted to be healthy were told that they must decrease
the amount of fat they were eating. Then, here comes a major
study that says the exact opposite.

While I don't want to get into the merits of that particular
study, it does reveal that in this life, truth can feel like a moving target—literally. People think doing one thing will make
them healthy, and the next day conventional wisdom says
otherwise. It doesn't take long to realize that the world is not
a very healthy place, and there aren't many solid answers for
how to make it better.

The same is true spiritually. In a quest for spiritual
health—a quest to satisfy inner hunger—where have spiritually unhealthy people turned? Where have they sought
more lasting answers for cultivating a healthy, vital life?
Many have sought answers exactly where they should: the

Church. Yet, what have they found there? In many cases, they have found a collection of unhealthy behaviors and sick individuals. Certainly, there are many wonderful, vibrant, healthy churches, but what is the average person experiencing from the church community as a whole? Most see a conflicted, unhealthy system.

And no wonder. Over lunch, Dr. Walter Kaiser, the former President of Gordon-Conwell Theological Seminary recently told me of his concerns for this very problem—along with one of the symptoms:

> *"What disturbs me so much is that our data shows 1,500 clergy are leaving the ministry each month—each month—and the cause in over half of those cases has something to do with either internet pornography or infidelity."*

That's just one example, but the reality is the church's leaders are leaving the church. Christians divorce at the same rate as the rest of the population. Episcopalians have ordained a homosexual bishop, causing a deep rift in that denomination. The Roman Catholic Church has been rocked by ongoing allegations of child sexual abuse among its priests. Recently, the pastor of one of the nation's largest Presbyterian congregations resigned amid allegations of sexual impropriety with a member of his staff. Cases of financial mismanagement and poor financial accountability are rampant. To make matters worse, many people base their opinions of "church leaders" on what they see on television, which unfortunately is often marked by showmanship, pleas for money, and an aggressively presented notion that God is about our personal prosperity. Many people want to get healthy, but in many cases, the church is not providing solid answers.

The result is that many people do not trust or respect the church. It hardly seems to be a place to find answers. Disillusioned, they yearn for something—anything—that feels authentic and real. They want to find God, but they want to find Him in an intimate and personal way. Sound familiar?

When I graduated from college and began job hunting, my life began to spiral downward. I loved God. I had what I considered to be a deep faith, yet I was not finding the satisfying life that I wanted. God seemed to be unable

God able to
not able to

to hear my prayers or simply uninterested in answering. This perception led to a growing anxiety regarding my life and my future. That anxiety gave birth to intense feelings of uncertainty and panic, which became panic attacks and eventually an all out panic disorder. A prisoner of my own mind, I remember searching for help and for answers, utterly confused at how this could happen to someone like me, someone with real faith.

During this time, I began listening to one preacher in particular. He captured me because he seemed to have a different style than most. He was not showy or particularly handsome, but he seemed to know just what I needed to hear and had a completely honest presentation. I loved his approach and his candid recognition of life's hard realities. He appeared to have it all figured out, and his faith gave me faith. Until, that is, news of his infidelity was made public. This man of God who proclaimed the truth had been involved in a decades-long sexual affair. In addition, he had played fast and loose with his expense account, taking thousands of dollars from his church for his supposed professional use. I was crushed.

In the ensuing days, the pastor was interviewed by several reporters and multiple stories were published detailing his condemning behaviors. I was startled to learn that, despite appearances, this man was wracked by self-doubt, filled with feelings of insignificance and hopelessly stumbling towards the end of his life. Isolated from others, he had carried his burdens alone, unable to let others glimpse his private hell.

Watching this man fall was devastating to me in two ways. First, he had not been real. He had not been authentic. I knew he wasn't perfect nor did I expect him to be. I did, however, trust that he was representing his relationship with God in an authentic way, and when I found out he wasn't, my tailspin deepened. If I could not trust this gifted, outwardly God-fearing man, then who in the church could I trust? Secondly, I was troubled by an even more disturbing thought: If this pastor was experiencing such pain and doubt, then what must many others in his church be going through? In other words, if a man whose job was to seek the face of God in Scripture can be wracked by such self-doubt and personal isolation, then imagine the state of the people sitting in the pews. And I knew I was one of them.

The lesson I learned then, and one I am still learning even now is this: I cannot put my trust in any other man or woman, pastor or lay person. The church is, by definition, an imperfect institution. We are all sinful people, but when infused by the Holy Spirit, God can use us as instruments in His Church. However, sometimes our sin gets the best of us, and Christ's Church becomes very messy. We should not be surprised by this. It's just how it works. Thus, we have to be sure that our focus is always on Christ, and never on a person. In my search for spiritual health, I needed to be in the church, among God's people, but I should not have been looking to them to find my sufficiency and healing. What I had to find was a way to cultivate my relationship with Christ in such a way that He was sufficient. He was, and continues to be, the only One who can make me well.

Although this pursuit needed to take place in the church, for that is His earthly body, I needed to create a model of living in my own life and ministry that removed people from pedestals, including my own. I needed to communicate a clear message in my life and ministry: "Don't look at me—look at Christ." In the church, through God's people, I could look to Christ. Despite imperfections, God can use us—regular people—as His instruments and vessels. What a joyous revelation! And just like that, I was freed to let people be themselves without feeling let down or betrayed. They—like me—were on a journey to Christ. In that way, I could be honest with all that I encountered.

Don't get me wrong—this kind of living is hard. All of us possess an unwillingness to live authentically in the midst of others. That's natural. No one wants to reveal their flaws and shortcomings. However, if we are not willing to be honest about our illness, how can we ever expect to get better? Especially in the church, we need to be authentic about who we are and our need for greater "health" in Christ. I recently spoke candidly to our congregation:

> "We have got to learn to get over ourselves. We all have the appearance of a good life, but we all know that is an illusion. We need to be real. So let's just get it over with. Turn to the person on your right and left and say, 'I'm not perfect, I have problems.'"

There was a big laugh, but I think I made my point. If we're going to get healthy, we need to find churches that are willing to accept us as we are, but even more than that, call us to new life in Christ.

A View From the Inside

Do such churches exist? Not an easy question to answer. Like many things, the answer is both yes and no. If the church is filled with sin-sick people, then yes, you will have some related illness. The church is never going to be perfect. However, the church should show evidence of the hope of the Gospel. By that I mean we should be able to see the transforming grace of God at work, redeeming broken hearts and bringing renewal and abundance to those who seek Him.

As a pastor for 19 years, I have had a first-hand look at his Bride, and what I have found is a gaping chasm between the faith that people talk about and the faith they actually live. I have found a disturbing disconnect between what people say they believe and what they actually experience. I have found a large disparity between what people think life can be and what it actually is. I have encountered very few people who actually seem to be living the "abundant life" that the Apostle John talks about in John 10:10.

This is not to suggest that I think Christians are to lead a perfect life. We are called to be holy, yes. It should be our heart's desire. However, our sinful nature still reigns. We should hear Paul's words echoing from Romans 7:15: "The things I want to do, I do not do; and the things I don't want to do, that's what I wind up doing. Deliver me from this body of death!" The reality is we are all broken people. That's why we're in church in the first place, isn't it? We are drawn to church because we know we are broken and we know we need a Savior.

Unfortunately, I find many people who occupy a pew on Sundays but finding no connection between that experience and the rest of their lives. They say they believe, but there is little joy. Paul nailed it when, referring to Sunday morning church goers, he said to Timothy, "having a form of godliness but denying its power..." It seems there is an abundance of people experiencing a form of godliness—the practice of religion—but they are not experiencing God's true transforming power.

Many years ago, I sat down with a husband and wife, active church members, who had it all. Rusty and Sharon were the couple everyone admired and wanted to emulate. Rusty was successful in his business, well-known in the community, and volunteered for numerous organizations and charities, not to mention the church. Sharon was the consummate wife and mother: athletic, attractive and organized, seemingly living above the fray. Nothing frazzled her. As I sat there across from them in my office, I could not help but think, "These people have got it together." But quickly, I discovered that was actually the farthest thing from the truth. I casually asked how they were doing, and when they each gave each other a blank stare, I knew that something was significantly wrong.

"We're having some trouble," Rusty said.

I then asked about their walk with Christ, which elicited more blank looks.

Soon their faces were flush with embarrassment. Sharon said, "I feel like we have created this life, but it feels like it's all a lie. We have been doing all these things because we feel like we're supposed to, but we're not happy, we're not happy with each other, and it's starting to take a toll." As the new house they were building rose from the ground, the family inside was crumbling. How could this happen? They had flatlined. No vital signs. They were doing a lot, but none of it gave them a deep, meaningful spiritual life in Christ.

Inside them both was a deep-seated insecurity that they sought to resolve through worldly accomplishments and visibility. It was as if they were trying to prove to themselves and the world that they were healthy by doing all the things the world expected. The result was a train wreck. They were empty, lost, alone, depressed and living under the weight of worldly expectations. Sadly, this is very familiar territory for many, even inside the church. Isak Dinesen, in her marvelous novel, *Out of Africa*, wrote:

> "Pride is faith in the idea that God had when He made us....Most people who have no pride are not aware of any idea God had in the making of them, and sometimes they make you doubt that there ever has been much of an idea, or else it has been lost—and who shall find it again? They have got to accept as success what others warrant to be,

*and to take their own happiness, and even their own selves,
at the quotation of the day. They tremble with reason before
their fate."*

We live in a culture in which most people have been
trained to assess their worth and value—their health as human beings—according to what others say, according to the
"quotation of the day." Indeed, such a fate leaves us trembling
at its stunning emptiness.

No one is exempt from this reality including those of us
who live out our professional lives inside the church. The
false notion that you and I must march to the world's drum
in order to prove our worth can be consuming. No one is exempt from the possibility of being sucked into its vortex. We
hear about the love and grace of God. We read about it in His
Word. We are inside the church. We are part of the Christian
community, and yet we're still not healthy. We're still sick, not
experiencing anything resembling abundant life.

Hope for a Healthy Future
So, where does that leave us? It leaves us feeling insecure and
anxious about our lives and our future. Even so, I do not believe we need to live that way. God has given us the answer,
and He has given it to us in Jesus Christ. When Jesus called
the disciples in Mark 3, it says, "He appointed twelve—des-
ignating them apostles—that they might be with Him...and
that He might send them out to preach."

As Jesus unfolded His plan to redeem and save the world,
He first enlisted those who would help Him lead, flawed com-
moners who simply chose to follow Him. Knowing that they
would be leading long after He was gone, it was imperative
that He establish their leadership in a way that would keep
them healthy over the long haul. What was the first ingredient? Jesus. He called them to Himself. The first leaders were
called to simply *be* with Jesus. Therein lies the key.

We have become so busy—both inside and outside of the
church—that no one has time to be with Jesus. It is from that
intimate relationship that His abundant life is poured into us,
but no one has time to allow that to happen. We have adopted
a "fast food" spiritual life. We need real nutrition, but there is
no time; McDonalds will have to do. We need spiritual meat,

ish prayer will have to do...hardly enough to keep us
.y over the long haul.

.n a sermon on the prodigal son, Charles Spurgeon, the
at Baptist preacher of the 19th Century, reminded his congregation that the Prodigal father ran down the road "and kissed him." The sermon was called, "The Kiss of the Father," and Spurgeon went on to say:

> *"Some of us know what it is like to be too happy to live. The love of God has been so overpoweringly experienced by us on some occasions that we almost have to ask God to stop the delight because we could endure no more. If God had not shielded His love and glory a bit, we believe we could not have stood it."*

When is the last time you felt like that? When is the last time you sensed the presence of God so deep and so full that you could hardly stand it? When have you ever had to ask God to stop the delight? Even as a pastor, getting to this place is a huge challenge. I am not naturally skilled at being with Him. I imagine you can identify with this challenge.

This kind of intimacy with God requires time and intentionality. It's a dimension to our spiritual lives that you and I have found easy to omit in favor of more culturally acceptable means of relationship. We want things that happen fast. In our world today, we can organize life around the quick, easy and impersonal. Instant messaging and text messages can easily become our primary mode of communication. We ask and we get an immediate answer. We know little about listening. We know little about *being*. We don't have to bother with the trappings of community. These patterns are at the root of what make is making us unhealthy.

It is my fervent prayer that this book will provide some insight into how you and I can conquer this epidemic illness, for no one is immune.

The good news is that, after being a pastor for nearly 20 years in three different churches, I have seen the signs of life that point to a healthy, vital relationship with Christ. I have seen the essential elements that lead to healthy, growing disciples of Jesus Christ—and healthy, growing congregations.

What I will share does not come from my own expertise. It comes from learning at the feet of Jesus. You and I can get healthy. And our healing will impact our churches. If we are willing to invest the time it takes to cultivate a new way of relating to our Savior, a vital walk with Christ the Lord can be ours.

2

*"All of us also lived among them at one time,
gratifying the cravings of our sinful nature and
following its desires and thoughts."*

EPHESIANS 2:3

*There was a time when meadow, grove and stream,
The earth, and every common sight,
To me did seem
Apparell'd in celestial light,
The glory and the freshness of a dream.
It is not now as it hath been of yore;
Turn wheresoe'er I may,
By night or day,
The things which I have seen I now can see no more.*

WILLIAM WORDSWORTH, ODE

Preaching my first sermon remains one of the greatest moments of my life and one of my sweetest memories. I was young—only 25 at the time—and naïve about the realities of serving in ministry. With one year at Austin Presbyterian Seminary under my belt, I was full of new ideas about what God was doing in the world and how He would use me.

I had just completed my first course in preaching—or as we Presbyterians call it, homiletics. For whatever reason, my professor made it sound like I was baking a cake or fixing a car or solving an equation. All I had to do was use the right ingredients or plug in the correct formula and *voila*—I had a sermon! The educational process felt rote and heavy, far from the spiritual experience I believed "preaching" should be.

The sermons we preached to one another in class seemed more like academic exercises (which they were) than experiences of God's transforming Word infused by the Holy Spirit. It seemed like we were working in a laboratory, and as such, it felt like a completely empty exercise. However, I was pleased to discover that having completed that course, I was allowed to sign up to preach on "the circuit." The seminary, located in central Texas, was within driving distance of a collection of small rural churches that could not afford full-time pastoral leadership. Those churches were thrilled to have seminary students come and preach, regardless of their experience. As a student who dreamed about preaching to his own congregation one day, I was grateful for the opportunity.

It was the first Sunday in June, 1989, when I preached my first official sermon. Armed with my Bible and my sermon notes, I headed west about 250 miles to the little town of Juno. I drove past the rolling hills of West Texas to a little postcard-worthy church, complete with tumbleweeds. Driving up, it was as if I'd found myself inside a Norman Rockwell painting: the small, white clapboard building and the steeple rising confidently toward the sky. It seemed an oasis in the middle of a dry land. And for those who came to worship there, that's exactly what it was.

However, in spite of the picturesque setting, I could feel my stomach churning. I was nervous about this "first" in my life and was anxious to get started. Walking into the church, I immediately discovered two things: first, the building had no air conditioning. On a hot and humid summer morning in Texas, it was already about 90 degrees in the sanctuary without a whisper of moving air. Secondly, my "congregation" was made up of eight elderly African-American women. As a suburban-born-and-bred white man, well, it was a cross-cultural experience I wasn't expecting!

Within minutes, I had been warmly welcomed and greeted by the ladies and we prepared to worship. Wanting to coordinate our singing for the morning, I went to the chancel, looking for the organist. Another problem: No organist. In fact—no organ. Deep breath. Not knowing what else to do, I picked up the hymnal and led the singing. To say that I was operating "outside of my gift set" would be an understatement; more like a plumber performing brain surgery. It was the first time I had ever tried something like that—and my last. Why those ladies didn't leave, I'm still not sure. It was awful.

Thoroughly discouraged, I went to the pulpit, opened my Bible, and began to preach. About five minutes into my message, sweat had soaked through my starched white shirt, my red silk "preaching tie" and was making its way completely through my navy suit. There was no getting around it—desperate times call for desperate measures. Without missing a word, I slid off my jacket, pulled off my shirt and tie, and preached the rest of my message wearing my suit pants and a white T-shirt. As I did, the women shouted a chorus of "Amens" which, being fully suburban and fully white, I wasn't quite sure what to do with. At the very least, I figured that having shed my heavy suit coat and shirt, the odds were better that I would remain conscious for the duration of my first sermon.

As my message unfolded, weak and halting as it was, the eight African-American church ladies—my congregation—acted as if they were listening to Billy Graham. They laughed at every joke, they cried at every story, they nodded their heads and said "Yes, Jesus!" to every point I tried to make. In short, they welcomed the Word of God with great thanksgiving in their hearts, as bread to someone who was starving.

Even more than their spontaneous affirmation of my sermon, I'll never forget how they welcomed me as their son. When I finished, each one hugged my neck and shook my hand and talked about Jesus. Each one looked me squarely in the eye and thanked me for sharing the Word with them that day. They weren't worried about the great difference in our ages or that my exegesis was far from perfect. They didn't care that I had sweat through my suit. They weren't focused on the color of my skin, the balance in my checkbook nor the make and model of my car. The only thing that mattered to them was that they had been given the gift of worship and the Word, and they were immensely grateful.

As I drove home that afternoon, I knew that those eight African-American women had just illustrated exactly what the people of God should be: free, unencumbered, focused on worship and the Word of God, filled with love and warmth for each other. That's it! This was the Church at her finest, and I was so grateful to have experienced it.

Since that day, I have encountered many churches large and small; congregations young and old; settings both rural and urban; and every kind of worship style imaginable.

Sadly, I have yet to find a church quite like that first one in Juno. I know it is a memory now and I'm likely romanticizing that hot summer day, but still, most churches—most Christian communities—are far from achieving the success of that simple model.

In many respects, God's people have melted into a frayed mess of denominations, institutional structures, high-profile personalities, and ever-growing political bureaucracies, marked by unending and polarizing theological debate. Rather than being a significant and vibrant part of mainstream American culture, the Church has become a peripheral influence hanging around the edges. To borrow from Wordsworth, "the things which I have seen I now can see no more."

Identifying the Illness
Think about it. When you hear about what God's people are doing these days, what leaps to mind?

For many, it is not a positive image: repeated instances of pastors failing morally, tragic cases of child abuse, misappropriation and mismanagement of funds, embezzlement, same-sex unions, and little or no personal discipline. As a result, people often view Christians as those trying to manipulate or prey upon others.

Perhaps the most stinging accusation of all is that the people of God are benign, void of any actual significance or relevance to a rapidly changing culture. How is that possible? How do we—people who have been given a spirit of power and not fear—become indifferent to those around us? I would rather be *anything* but benign.

While there is probably more than one reason why the Church falls so short, much of it can be traced to the fact that we have become seriously ill. There's a malignancy in us, and it's multiplying rapidly, draining our power and depriving the Body of Christ of the life that God longs to give us.

Thankfully, this is not the first time God's people have suffered through this. In fact, it was this same illness Paul addressed when he wrote his letter to the Ephesian Christians. Much like the Christians of today, the believers in Ephesus were a pretty mixed up, messy bunch, but Paul was not willing to let them stay that way. He challenged them. He encouraged them. He taught them. He started his letter by encouraging the believers to come together as one body in order to create a ministry that was glorifying to God. He prayed in the first chapter that the "eyes of their hearts would be enlightened" such that they might know hope and glory and power. This is one of the truly great prayers in the Bible.

Then, in Chapter 2, Paul makes a dramatic sh
that before we can know hope and glory and peac
face the harsh reality of our own sickness. Paul
Ephesians 2:3:

> *"All of us lived among the disobedient at one time, g ..*
> *fying the cravings of our sinful nature and following its*
> *own desires and thoughts. Like the rest, we were by nature*
> *objects of wrath."*

In order to truly understand and experience what the
Christian life is all about, Paul says we must come to grips
with our sin and its consequences: alienation from God. If we
want to fulfill our deepest desires and embrace the abundant
life, then we must examine the condition of our hearts. (John
10:10) It's not pretty. The dark nature of the human heart
causes us to live looking out for number one—*our* wants, *our*
needs, *our* desires—and so we alienate ourselves from others. That same sin calls down the wrath of God, separating
us from our Creator. Paul could not be more clear about the
plight of the human condition—and he's right.

Need more evidence? Just look around you. Consider
what is happening in the world and the trajectory of our culture. You don't have to spend a long time reading up on current events to realize that humanity has a serious problem. I
won't bore you with specifics—you know what I'm talking
about. Naturally, we've tried to assign blame in a variety of
different places, but there's something missing from our analysis. The things we see happening in our world could not be
our fault, could they? Surely not! Richard Schweder, professor
of comparative human development at the University of Chicago wrote in the *New York Times*:

> *"The world woke up from the slumber of the dark ages, fi-*
> *nally got in touch with the truth and became "good" about*
> *300 years ago in Northern and Western Europe. As people*
> *opened their eyes, religion (equated with ignorance and su-*
> *perstition) gave way to science (equated with fact and rea-*
> *son). Unfortunately, as a theory of history, that story has*
> *had a predictive utility of approximately zero. At the turn*
> *of the millennium it was pretty hard not to notice that the*
> *20th century was probably the worst one yet, and that the*

big causes of all the death and destruction had rather little
to do with religion."

Oh yes, many years ago we decided we were good. We didn't need "religion" to make us feel guilty about our shortcomings. We moved our faith aside and came up with some other reasons to justify the ills of the world. People thought it was possible to alter the environments in which we lived, the education we received, the technology we used, and the politics we employed and somehow make the world better.

However, in the end, where did it get us? Back to square one. We can no longer escape the fact that the problem is not "out there." The genesis of the problem hits way closer to home; the problem is the *human heart.* Christianity is the sole theology of all the religions in the world that has a rational, reasoned explanation as to what we see happening in the world. Humanity, by nature, is selfish, and without intervention, on a one-way path to certain and lasting destruction.

Me? Sick? No!

My wife and I have three children, John David, Alex and Kaylee. They are now teenagers, but when they were little, we went through a number of years in which at least one of them was always sick. We beat an almost constant path to our pediatrician's door such that I felt certain we would be honored with some kind of VIP status, perhaps our own monogrammed chair or dedicated exam room.

One particularly bad winter, over a four-week period, each of our children had strep throat not once, but twice. They would get sick, take their medicine and get better, but within days, they were sick again. To make matters worse, even Leigh came down with strep, and I can assure you, when Mom gets sick, our house as we know it implodes. Everything comes to a screeching halt.

In spite of my exhaustion, I was feeling quite smug about the fact that I was the only member of the family strong enough to fight off this illness. "What a bunch of weaklings I live with," I thought. Good, old-fashioned pride.

Towards the end of the second round of infections, I dutifully loaded my entire sick family in the car and took them back to the doctor for yet another examination, another bill, and more expensive medicine. However, as I sat with my children during their exams, my bravado was deflated when the doctor asked, "David, have you been tested for strep?"

"What? Me? Why would I get tested? I'm the only one in this family functioning properly. What is this guy talking about?" I didn't say that of course, and instead simply muttered, "No. Why would I do that?"

"Well," he said, "You may be the one infecting everyone else. Sometimes you can have strep but not be symptomatic, which is actually quite dangerous." I shrugged it off as a doctor struggling for an explanation to something he couldn't diagnose, and went home with my air of superiority in tact.

Unfortunately, my wife had heard the doctor's warning and for the next 48 hours, I was reminded of all the reasons why I should be tested. Even so, I still maintained complete innocence. There was *no way* I was sick.

However, in spite of my best efforts, my wife finally wore me down. Just to prove her wrong once and for all, I went to my internist and got a strep test. When he came back to the examination room following the test, the look on his face said it all. Much to my chagrin, I *was* sick. I was the carrier, and I had been repeatedly infecting my family.

Ouch. I was sick, but my stubborn indignation prevented me from even considering the notion, much less admitting and resolving the problem. As a result, the people around me—the ones I loved the most—had suffered. I humbly slinked home with my antibiotics to tell my family that, sure enough, I was the culprit.

In so many ways, I think the notion of our own "goodness" is the curse of our culture. Popular humanist thinking celebrates the power and goodness of the self. We see the pain, brokenness and wounds all around us, but we have been taught to arrogantly assume, "It's not me. I'm not the problem. I'm fine." All the while, we are infecting those around us, especially those we love, because we are unwilling to assume any responsibility for who we are or what we are doing. It seems like no one is willing to take responsibility for anything because no one ever wants to admit they've done anything wrong.

"It's not *my* fault," we say, as we search frantically for a place to cast our blame. We don't want to believe that the problem may begin and end with us.

Sure, we may hear what Paul says about sin and nod our heads in agreement but—just like me in the doctor's office—

we still don't want to talk about it. After all, who wants to talk about their imperfections? What's more, while we know what God says about sin, we're still not totally convinced it's true. Do we honestly think we're sinful? Do we really believe there is something wrong with us? Isn't there a voice in the back of your head, which occasionally whispers, "Wait a second— you ARE a good person!"

How we settle this internal debate may determine everything about our future health. In his book, *Knowing God*, J.I. Packer wrote:

> "*Modern man...with all his achievements naturally inclines to a rather high opinion of himself. In the moral realm, he is resolutely kind to himself, treating small virtues as compensating for great vices and refusing to take seriously the idea that, morally speaking, there is anything much wrong with him.*"

Isn't that exactly what we do? We think as long as we keep the scales of right and wrong tipping slightly in our favor, we've achieved a good life. We're using the ledger system, trying to keep our accounts in balance by using little virtues to equal out our larger vices. We know we've let our spouse down or disappointed our children, so we write a check to a charity and consider the scales of virtue and vice squared away. We move about comparing ourselves to the goodness we see in others and—being kind to ourselves—decide we're doing okay. Deep down, we believe that God must grade on a curve and all we have to do is finish in the top half to get to heaven.

We think, "Well, I may not be as holy as Mother Theresa, but I'm a lot better than my neighbor." With the right comparison, we can convince ourselves we're still in the top half of the world on the goodness scale, pat ourselves on the back and pronounce ourselves fit for heaven.

While that may sound good for a time, we need to test our own analysis. We have actually set up a flawed system because our standards are faulty. The method by which we measure our goodness is wrong. We're using the world's standard for goodness and holiness and not the standard set out for us by God. His standard is nothing less than the holiness of His nature, a nature revealed in the perfect character of His Son, Jesus Christ. There isn't any wiggle room in that standard. He said, "Be holy, as I am holy." (Leviticus 19:2)

The only way we will ever understand the true nature of our hearts is to reflect on the true nature of God's holiness. When we do that, there is a cause and effect to that understanding. When we realize who God is in His holiness, we become acutely aware of who we are *not*. When we honestly examine God's nature, we will inevitably come to the same conclusion: we have been sickened by sin and we need help. As M. Basil Pennington writes in *Thomas Merton: Brother Monk*:

> *"We are broken persons and live in broken communities in a state of brokenness. We are alienated from ourselves and from each other. We do not readily fit together. We are like a bunch of porcupines trying to huddle together for warmth who are always driven apart out of fear of the wound we can inflict upon each other with our quills."*

Discipline

Learning to be the Patient

So, what's the answer? As is often the case, the first step toward healing is acknowledging we are sick. We must accept that we need help. Without that simple, yet profound recognition, we will never seek nor understand the help being offered to us by the Great Physician.

Imagine this with me for a moment. You are a pedestrian. You are walking home from work and as you cross the street, you look up and there is a car barreling towards you. You freeze. There is nothing you can do. You're going to be hit. Then, out of nowhere, someone comes up from behind and miraculously knocks you out of the way. You hit the ground hard and all your belongings scatter, but while you are examining your scrapes and bruises, you realize—you're alive!

What's your reaction? Naturally, you leap to your feet and throw your arms around the neck of the person who knocked you out of the way. You thank him profusely. You offer to pay him for his daring. You feel deeply obligated to him for the risk he took in saving your life. You will never forget him.

Now, imagine the same scene, only this time, you don't see the car. The same man comes up from behind and knocks you out of the way. The car speeds past but you never see it. Your things go flying as you fall down. You are scraped and bruised, and have no idea what just happened. How are you going to react this time? More than likely, fuming, you will get up, dust yourself off and find the man who knocked you down to give him a piece of your mind.

In the second case, the man was nothing more than a nuisance to you—a troubling annoyance who complicated your life. You would have no appreciation for his risk nor the fact that your life was spared. Of course, this is the scene that unfolds around us every day. Rarely do people see the car.

There's something powerful, relentless, and unyielding heading straight for us. We are powerless to get out of the way without help. The question is: do we see the car? If we do, then the work of Christ becomes something for which we are deeply grateful. However, if we don't, if we live refusing to believe there is anything wrong with us, then the work of Christ or any mention of it will be nothing more than a persistent annoyance, a nuisance we must learn to ignore throughout the course of our lives.

If we're ever going to achieve vitality in our Christian lives and experience the abundance which God promises, we have to see the car. We have to recognize that sin has the power to destroy us. We must be willing to admit we are sick and we need healing. The moment we do, that is the moment when everything changes. When we see the car, we finally fall in love with the person who came to knock us out of the way. When we see the car is when we see Jesus.

In Ephesians 2:13, Paul writes: "But now in Christ Jesus you who were once far away (alienated) have been brought near through the blood of Christ." Humanity was in a pit so deep, we could not save ourselves. In the midst of that darkness, Christ came to bleed and die—to bear the penalty for our sin—so that we might have reconciliation, redemption and abundant life. He knocked us out of the way in order that he would bear the oncoming punishment. God willingly sacrificed the life of His Son, allowing the Son to become the object of the Father's wrath instead of us.

To be clear, the blood of Christ is not optional. Acts 4:12 reminds us there is but one name under heaven by which we may be saved, and it is the name of Jesus Christ. Our culture is famous for dismissing the truth of our faith with an arrogant wave of the hand. They say, "Oh, Christianity is so exclusive. They think they have cornered the market on truth." Such a statement could not be farther from the truth. Christianity is the most inclusive religion in the world in that *all* people are invited to come to Christ. No one is excluded from that invitation, and they are invited to come just as they are.

While it would be easy and convenient to say that all religions are equally valid, here's the deal: there are theological ramifications, if we allow for more than one road to salvation. When Jesus was in the garden, praying to God and asking, "If there is any other way, take this cup from me," don't you think God would have prevented His Son from suffering if there was another way? (Matthew 26:39) If Jesus' death was avoidable in any way, don't you think the Father would have said, "Great news, my Son, Buddhism is also truth! Islam works! They are paths that will reconcile the world to me! You don't have to die!"

But that's not what He said, is it? No, Jesus went to the cross because it was the only way that the sin of our hearts could be cleansed and the wrath of God satisfied. If we choose to believe that Christ is but one of many ways to salvation, then God has just moved from being loving and gracious, to a cold and heartless murderer. With that understanding, He is now a God who kills his own Son for no reason. Either Jesus Christ is *the* way—or he is a lunatic, a nut case who wields no power or influence. The core of the Christian faith rises and falls on the cross and resurrection of Jesus. And the core of our faith—of your faith and mine—rests on our personal acknowledgement of our need for Him.

Further, simple logic tells us that two contradictory truths cannot both be true at the same time. People who say that all religions are equally valid show their own ignorance because that is quite impossible. Islam, which affirms that God would never become man, and Christianity, which affirms that God did become man, cannot both be true at the same time. It's one or the other. Our task, as Chuck Colson writes in his book, *How Now Shall We Live*, is to find out what is true and then to live in step with that truth. It is the truth that sets us free. It is the truth that heals us, the truth of Jesus Christ.

Life in the Hospital
The truth is we are sin-sick people in need of a savior, and there is freedom in recognizing and accepting that truth. We are the patients. In fact, this discovery—that we are sick and

that many others are infected as well—is the great blessing of our inclusion in the community of faith. It's a worldwide epidemic. Everyone has the same problem. Furthermore, the sick and needy gather on a regular basis in a "hospital" known as the Church. Our repentance and the expression of our trust in Christ open the door for the Church to be what God intended it to be: the divine creation of His earthly Kingdom.

The Church is not a man-made institution, but a divinely created vessel of God's own hand. Paul writes in Ephesians 2:19, "Consequently, you are no longer foreigners and aliens, but fellow citizens with God's people and members of God's household." In other words, every person who is touched by the Spirit—recognizing their own sin and God's work of redemption in Christ—is immediately welcomed into a community; they become part of God's people, part of His family of believers.

God intended the Church to be a home to everyone living in union with God *in* Christ. Look at Ephesians 2:21: "In Him, the whole building is joined together." Paul is painting a picture of the Church as a household, an earthly structure compelled into ministry by faith. Entrance into this household is determined by one thing and one thing only: union with Christ.

Clearly, this has a number of implications for us, but I will focus on just three:

First, the Church is not defined by a building or a charismatic leader; it is not defined by common political interests, a denomination or any other criteria outlined by humanity. When we get to heaven, there will not be a General Assembly meeting, a Pope or Anglican bishops. The Church of Jesus Christ exists outside time and space. In every time and every age, eternally, it is made up of all men and women who have found union with God in Christ by His cross and resurrection. It is the household of faith, limitless and timeless in its expression, not bound by human constructs.

Secondly, if we agree that the Church is the household of faith, then it raises the question, "How do we get in?" That is the heart of the matter—the question every individual must ask themselves. Far more significant than, "Am I a member of First Presbyterian Church?" is the larger, foundational question: "Am I a member of the one Church of Jesus Christ?"

This may sound somewhat surprising, but you don't join the Church by acknowledging the validity of a set of doctrinal principles or theological statements. You cannot be grandfathered in to church membership by family tradition, heritage, or influence. Signing a piece of paper or completing coursework does not make you a church member. You are a member of *the* Church—with a capital C—because you have had a life-changing, heart-transforming encounter with the redeeming love of Jesus Christ. You have come to terms with the darkness of your own heart, and found union with Him. *That* is how you get in.

In his commentary on Ephesians 2, John Stott wrote:

> *"What constitutes the distinctness of the members of God's new society? Not just that they admire or even worship Jesus, not just that they ascent to the dogmas of the church, not even that they live by certain moral standards. No, what makes them distinctive is their new solidarity as a people who are in Christ."*

Third, I think it is important to point out that it is possible for you to be a member of a church, but not be a member of *the* Church of Jesus Christ. Did you know that? One does not necessarily assume the other.

I spent five years as the pastor of a church in Ft. Myers, Florida. During my tenure, our congregation experienced a significant spiritual awakening. It was a privilege to see God working in individual lives as well as the church as a whole. When it came time for me to move on, and I had preached my final sermon, a dear couple, both faithful servants in the church, came up to me and said, "We were members of this church for 20 years before we knew who Christ was and why He died. The Gospel has changed our lives." They were members of Covenant Presbyterian Church *before* they were actually members of Christ's Church.

Once you commit yourself to Christ, it is important to find a body of believers with whom you can worship. We need the Church, that gathered community of faith, a community of brothers and sisters all infected with the same illness, a community in need of a savior. Local church membership has value; however, it is nothing until you have union with Christ and can claim membership in His Church.

Getting Out and Getting Home

Several months ago, a good friend of mine was flying from Atlanta to Jackson, Mississippi. Just after reaching cruising altitude the pilot came on the intercom with what seemed like the normal introductory remarks until he said, "Please pardon me as I deviate from my normal script here, but I want you to know that you have been granted both the privilege and the honor of escorting the body of Army PFC Jones (he could not remember the specific name) home tonight. PFC Jones was killed in Iraq fighting to extend the freedoms we enjoy to the people of that country. We are also accompanied by PFC Jones' cousin, Marine Major (name unknown), who has been chosen by the family to escort PFC Jones on his journey home."

As the gravity of the announcement sunk in, my friend said he was not quite sure what to do. As he tells it, there was utter silence for a few seconds, but then the whole plane burst into applause. In the moments that followed, the plane returned to a quiet reflective mood, and, according to my friend, it was as if each person was considering their journey—where they were, how far they had wandered from home—and hoping that one day, they too, might find their way back.

Something in all of us yearns for home. I love to just say the word "home." It flows off my tongue in such a soothing way. I think this longing is especially true when we're sick. No one wants to become ill when they're away from home. I had surgery several years ago, and while my stay in the hospital was only a week, it seemed much longer. I cannot tell you how good it felt to get out and get home.

I think that is what all of us are trying to do. We're trying to get out and get home. We are all on a journey in this life, a journey full of trials and struggles and hurt and pain. We must contend with questions and confusion, with the consequences of poor choices and individual failures. And to make matters worse—we're sick. However, in the midst of it all is the Church—a divinely-appointed body, flawed in every respect, but when filled by the Holy Spirit, a place of redemption and healing and hope; a community where, when lost, we can find not only ourselves, but also our path back home. In the words of John Stott:

"I wonder if anything is more urgent today, for the honor of Christ...than that the church should be, and should be seen to be, what by God's purpose and Christ's achievement it already is—a single new humanity, a model of human community, a family of reconciled brothers and sisters who love their Father and love each other, the evident dwelling place of God by His Spirit. Only then will the world believe in Christ as Peacemaker. Only then will God receive the glory due His name."

I can still vividly remember that old white clapboard church, rising from the middle of nowhere, and the faces of my first congregation—eight African-American women who came to worship. For just that moment, God gave me a glimpse of the hope of a new humanity—a family of reconciled brothers and sisters, the evident dwelling place of God.

Yes, we're sick, but we have seen the vision of health and wholeness. We must find our way back to that place that we know exists but from which we have been cut off. That place which is our heart's true home. If we can come to terms with the fact that we are lost, we will have taken the first step in finding our way back home.

> *Our birth is but a sleep and a forgetting:*
> *The soul that rises with us, our life's Star,*
> *Hath elsewhere its setting,*
> *And cometh from afar:*
> *Not in entire forgetfulness,*
> *And not in utter nakedness,*
> *But trailing clouds of glory do we come*
> *From God, who is our home...*
>
> – WILLIAM WORDSWORTH, ODE

3

(handwritten margin notes: "We don't use our perspectives!" and "✕ Discipline NO")

"I base what I do on what I feel is right or wrong. I work on the spur-of-the-moment thinking, and whatever my body wants to do, I do. Impulse is what I go by."

A TORONTO TEEN, YOUTH UNLIMITED MAGAZINE

"And He is the head of the body, the Church; He is the beginning and the firstborn from among the dead, so that in everything He might have the supremacy."

COLOSSIANS 1:18

I spent the first twelve years of my ministry working with students in various capacities; first as a Sunday School teacher, then as a Bible study leader, a full-time intern and finally, as an ordained youth pastor. For several reasons, I look back on those years as some of the most fruitful and enjoyable of my life.

First, I found students to be incredibly open and responsive to the Gospel in a way that most adults are not. Like sponges, they willingly soaked up the truth of Jesus. Secondly, you can get away with doing things in youth ministry that you could never pull off in any other area of life. For instance, in what other job can you throw overripe fruit at one another and have it considered a welcome activity? In what other job can you dress up like Elvis and run all over town? In what other job would people consider you "gifted" and "cool" for doing so? I rest my case.

One fall, while I was youth pastor at Signal Mountain Presbyterian Church, I took a group of about 125 high school students on a retreat to a little camp nestled outside the beautiful metropolis of Ten Mile, Tennessee. If you blink—you miss it. The fall in Tennessee is always very colorful, and this camp was gorgeous—a lake nearby, falling leaves, cool temperatures—it was perfect.

Unfortunately, the staff—like the rest of us in the Body—were not perfect. They were more like the "rules police." Grace was something they understood to be a prayer before meals. Their primary objective seemed to be preventing students from doing anything that could even remotely be considered fun. Even so, we were still managing to have a great time—enjoying the teaching and fellowship and beauty—and, as always, busy planning our late-evening activities. Middle-of-the-night adventures were part of our fall retreat tradition. They became part of the lore and legend that grew from year to year, thus attracting more students to attend. It was always the guy cabins versus the girl cabins as they tried to outwit one another by executing various pranks and raids. Trust me, these were not your average pranks. These pranks required a year's worth of meticulous planning and strategic analysis. Careful execution was imperative.

That night around 2 a.m., the girls struck first, breaking into our cabins and stealing our toiletry bags and towels. Fortunately, I had hidden a stash of shaving cream in my car, so after waiting an hour or two for the girls to settle back into their cabins, I led the boys on a raid of the girls' compound. Yes, I led 45 young men dressed in camouflage gear and blacked-out faces on a mission, sneaking through the woods. General Patton had nothing on me. We arrived at the girls' cabins, spied our targets, uncapped our cans, and made our move. We let loose with battle cries and whoops, ran down the hill and burst into their cabins, spraying shaving cream on anything that moved. Naturally, we assumed a quick, easy victory. But it was not to be. The girls had not gone to sleep empty handed. They rose from the dark shadows of their cabins armed with shaving cream as well, and our little raid soon poured out of the cabins into the surrounding woods and fields, an all-out shaving cream war. It was at that moment—that positively glorious moment—when the chaos was pierced by the loud, angry voice of the camp director: "Just what do you think you're doing? STOP. IT. STOP. IT. This behavior is not allowed here! Don't you know that shaving cream will kill the grass and plants? Who's in charge here? Where is your leader?"

Naturally, most of the students stopped dead in their tracks, sheepishly dropping the shaving cream cans from their hands. Heads bowed. All eyes turned to me. There I was, in army fatigues and a blackened face—guilty. Busted. If I could have found a hole to crawl in, I would have, but trying to be a responsible leader, I raised my hand and said, "Um…. that would be me. I'm the group leader."

"Well, you had better come with me," the director growled. "And as for the rest of you, start taking damp cloths and wiping the shaving cream off the grass and leaves." Needless to say, that was the end of our "fun" for the night, and I had the pleasure of sitting through a twenty minute lecture on the dangers of mixing shaving cream with green grass and leafy plants.

Who's In Charge?

That's the fundamental question, is it not? People in the world today, Christian and non-Christian alike, want to know who is in charge. It's a normal response. If you go to a restaurant and have a bad experience, you ask for the manager. You want to speak to the person in charge. Why? The person in charge should have the power to make things right. Let's say you go to a hotel and check in to a dirty, smelly room. When you step out into the hallway you find trays of half-eaten food and abandoned towels. Wouldn't you be asking yourself, "My goodness, who is running this place?" It is the right question to ask.

As we established in the last chapter, humanity is suffering with an illness. We're sick and no one seems to have a cure. It seems impossible to ignore the problem—the evidence is all around us. Violence. War. Abuse. Addiction. Crumbling marriages and families. Dishonest businesses. Shady political leaders. It's all there. The world is a mess. So, we turn to the church, Christ's Body, and what do we find there? We find the same illness. In many churches, regardless of denomination or economic status, there is confusion, dysfunction and chaos. To be sure, the Church, by definition, is a flawed place. When you put a bunch of sinful people together, it's going to get a little messy from time to time.

That said, I think an outside observer would be disheartened by what he sees. News about questionable behavior and scandals surrounding church leaders and ordained clergy is hard to avoid. In the denomination in which I serve—the PC (USA)—we have pastors who are openly defying church law and blessing same-sex unions. We even have pastors who openly question the Lordship of Jesus Christ and at some points, even deny it. We are spending thousands of dollars to support political causes, while at the same time cutting funding to missionaries in the field. Most alarmingly is the fact that we have lost more than 25,000 members a year for more than 20 years, and that's a conservative estimate. At our current rate, our denomination will cease to exist in 20 years. Now, I don't know about you, but that leaves me wondering, "Who's in charge around here? Who is the head of this church?"

A Secular Answer

When the question of who's in charge is posed to the culture, the answer we often receive is, "I am." Our culture has moved to an individualistic world view in which each person has authority and that authority is to be viewed as equal to everyone else. There is no "higher" authority to which every one must submit. There is no such thing as absolute truth. Thus, there is an almost infinite number of people or systems claiming authority or power or access to truth, and no one is allowed to believe that their truth is absolutely true. Such belief is viewed as being offensive to others.

Let me give you an example of what I am talking about. Several years ago, Rhonda Byrne wrote a very popular book called *The Secret*. It was a #1 *New York Times* bestseller for many weeks and now has more than 16 million copies in print in over 40 languages. Byrne says the "secret" to our happiness can be achieved in three words: ask, believe and receive. If you want something, ask for it, earnestly believe you'll get it—and presto—you'll have it! She calls it the "law of attraction." According to her book, the answer to the question of who's in charge is simple: we are. That's the secret.

I opened this chapter with the quote of a Toronto teenager who believes that she is in charge; that she is calling the shots. Honestly, why should she think otherwise? Our culture continually reinforces that message. However, the state of our world tells another story. With anyone and everyone claiming authority and power, the end result is total chaos. When everyone thinks they are in charge, then no one is in charge, and the result is chaos. Perhaps we need to keep searching for another answer.

If our search continues, at some point, we begin to look beyond the secular world into the spiritual realm. Could there be an answer there? If we think there might be, often, the first place we search is the Church. Biblically, the Church is not a man-made institution, but a divinely created household of faith made of up of all those who have ever found union with Christ by His blood; a universal community of all those who are *in* Christ—past, present, and future. That is what the Church is; it is not a building. It is not a place. It is the gathered community of faith. So if that is what the Church is, then how does it operate? Who is in charge? It is that question that drives us to Paul's letter to the Colossian church.

A Divinely Led Community
When something goes wrong, we want to know who's in charge because we believe they should be able to fix things. If we look to the Church for help and what we find is illness or trouble, then naturally we will ask, "Who has the ability to prescribe a remedy for this illness that will work?" The Colossian church was wrestling with these same questions when Paul wrote to help them understand where hope could be found.

Contextually, the Colossian church was very young and very troubled. As is mentioned in Colossians 1:7, this church had been under the ministry and teaching of Epaphras whom Paul describes as a faithful minister of the Lord. Paul believes Epaphras is faithfully presenting and proclaiming the Gospel of Jesus Christ. However, historically, we know that in addition to Epaphras, there were other teachers, teachers who were discounting Paul's teaching and promoting their own agendas. They were teaching that the Colossian church did not have the full measure or the full power of the Gospel. They tried to convince the church body that Epaphras had taken them as far as he could and presented themselves as clear authorities who could take the church to the next level of spiritual knowledge and power which had previously been unavailable to them.

As you can imagine, this created doubt and confusion in a spiritually young and relatively immature church. The Colossian Christians wanted to know the truth and whom they should believe. In essence, they were struggling with the issue of authority. Plain and simple, they needed to figure out who was in charge. Sound familiar?

One could argue that we, in 21st century America, are facing the same challenges and asking the same questions as the Colossian church all those years ago. Think about it. Are we witnessing any teaching in today's church suggesting that the Biblical and confessional standards of the church's past are now outdated? Are we being told that we need to be enlightened by a new contemporary, culturally conditioned theology? Are there teachers saying that what was true about human sexuality a few years ago is now outdated and irrelevant in a new cultural context? Are there any teachers in the church who are saying that salvation can be found apart from the work of Christ? I would say an emphatic, "Yes!" There are exactly those kinds of teachers at work among us which makes Paul's words all the more relevant to our situation today. If we are going to have a vital, healthy life in Christ and healthy, growing churches, we had better be clear about who's in charge.

The Head of the Church

First, the one, true and only head of the Church is Jesus Christ. There is none other. Who's in charge? Christ! To whose authority do we bow in submission? Christ! Paul states irrefutably in Colossians 1:16-18: "By Him all things were created... whether thrones or powers or rulers or authorities; all things were created by Him and for Him...*and He is the head of the Body, the Church*" (Italics mine.)

Paul paints a very clear picture. Christ is at the center of all things, the image of the invisible God. If all rulers and thrones and powers and authorities are subject to Him, then when it comes to the matter of the creation of God's new humanity, the Church, then He, too, is its singular head, the sufficient and supreme Lord of all. Christ is in charge. Period. It is not a matter up for debate or discussion. We do not need to form a committee to study it. It is not something we have to examine from multiple angles. The Body of the Church has one head and one head only—and it is Christ. (As an aside, this truth is revealed in Scripture, God's holy, inspired and infallible Word. If a person views the Bible as merely a book of wisdom, then I can understand why that person would find this argument untenable. I do not have time in this space to go into an explanation of the Authority of Scripture, but were I to be in conversation with such a person, I would argue from sources other than Scripture to point to the same truth, most notably, the historicity of the resurrection of Jesus Christ.)

Thus, let us be clear that no human construct can supersede the headship of Christ. The Pope of the Roman Catholic Church is not in charge. The bishops and archbishops of the Anglican Communion are not in charge. The General Assembly of any Reformed body is not in charge. The Annual Conference of United Methodists, the Southern Baptist Convention—none of these humanly created entities is in charge. In an earthly context, yes, they have some authority, but ultimately, they are not in charge. Christ is in charge. The head of any church that calls itself Christian, whether or not the church body understands, is Christ. He is in charge and as followers of Jesus Christ who hunger for health and vitality, we should do everything in our power to ensure that we remain under His headship and submissive to His authority.

It follows then, that because He is in charge, He is the only one who can truly make a difference. He is the only one who can bring about transformation. He is the one who can heal our sickness. He prescribes the medicine. Our problem, of course, is we stubbornly refuse to listen. We don't want to hear His prescription. We don't follow Him or, if we do, it is short-lived. We quickly return to our own brand of headship, living apart from the counsel of God and thus reaping the consequences of our sin. I know this sounds simple, but if we want to live vital, healthy abundant lives in Christ, we need to do what we're told. Paul writes in 1 Thessalonians 4:1, "Finally, brothers, we instructed you how to live in order to please God..." What pleases God? Our obedience. God is pleased when we simply follow His instructions and do what He says. If someone is in charge, this seems to be a completely rational expectation, doesn't it?

Several months ago, while playing basketball, I planted my foot to cut left and suddenly felt like I had been shot in the leg. My left calf was torn and it was without a doubt the worst injury I have ever sustained. I went to the doctor that afternoon and after an exam and x-rays he prescribed the following: wear a black plastic boot for three weeks, followed by eight weeks with no activity beyond walking, after which I would need to be examined again. No golf. No basketball. No running. I was not happy, but I dutifully put on my boot and went home.

I wore the boot for about three days and the pain gradually subsided. With the pain gone, my stereotypical male stubbornness kicked in and I decided I didn't need to follow the doctor's advice in order to heal. I would not wear the boot, but instead walk gingerly and carefully. Surely that wouldn't cause any further problems. Surprise, surprise—I was wrong. Within hours, my leg got worse. I called the doctor two days later convinced something else had gone wrong. Sure enough, his first question was whether or not I was wearing the boot and you can bet I got a gentle tongue lashing for my disobedience. The doctor made it clear that he was in charge and if I wanted to get better, I had to learn to follow his instructions.

Why would we expect anything different from God? We have a problem. We're sick. Even so, we have the right prescription. Thankfully, we have a Creator who knows us intimately and personally. He has shown us the path of life, the remedy for sin, and commanded us to walk in it. However, we are stubbornly refusing to do as we are told, believing we can come up with a better remedy on our own. And how is that working out for us? Lousy. Evidence of our failed attempts at control are all around us. While trying to be in charge, we are getting progressively sicker as we blindly wonder, "How could this be happening?" Much like the counsel of my doctor, if we truly want to get better, we must learn to listen to the Great Physician and do as we are told. We need to be obedient.

A Distinctive Headship
Human nature being what it is, even when we know we need to be obedient, we struggle to do so. We keep looking for our own remedies because we lack the basic trust that someone else can adequately handle our issues. As odd as it might sound, we're just not sure God is going to take care of us the right way, at least the way we think He should. We wonder if He can really fulfill His promises. Is He that powerful?

In the summer of 2004, I had accepted a call to First Presbyterian Church in Orlando and was busy trying to conclude my ministry in Ft. Myers, and working out the details of moving my family. I had a contract to sell my house in Ft. Myers and another to buy a house in Orlando. We had movers lined up and schools picked out for our children, and just when things felt under control, Hurricane Charlie came calling.

Blowing in from the Gulf of Mexico, Charlie—a Category Four storm—devastated much of southwest Florida, leaving many without homes and thousands more without power. Weakening slightly to a Category Two, Charlie took dead aim at Orlando and brought widespread damage to that city, though thankfully less than what the coast had experienced. Our new house, that I was contractually obligated to purchase, was damaged. The church in Ft. Myers was a mess. The house I was selling in Ft. Myers, but had not closed on, was damaged. I was supposed to be moving in ten days, and yet I felt responsible for ministering to the hurting Ft. Myers community. The final indignity was that, in the midst of it all, no one had power. As a result, it was nearly impossible to get anything accomplished. You couldn't charge your cell phone. You couldn't keep food in the refrigerator. You couldn't cook. You couldn't cool off. It was miserable.

Looking back, however, I learned a valuable lesson. The longer we lived in the dark, the more I noticed a particular disorder arising. I called it "power envy." Nearly every conversation you had with another human being began with the words, "Do you have power yet?" If the answer was yes, you felt a strange twinge of envy bordering on anger. If you had gotten your power back, you felt an odd sense of guilt about it. You almost felt the need to apologize or invite them to come live with you. After seven days, when the power trucks finally appeared at the end of our block, I cried. I know—ridiculous. Even so, I have never been so glad to see two men and a truck as I was that day.

I believe the "power envy" dynamic has direct application to our understanding of the headship of Christ and the authority of Jesus. Unlike those who have been hit by a storm, we who claim the name of Jesus are *never* going to be without power. And not just any power, a robust power, strong enough to handle whatever life may throw at us. We will never need to envy the power of others because no one will have a power greater than ours.

The indwelling power of God is a power both supreme and sufficient. Paul writes in Colossians 1:18, "...in everything, Christ is supreme." This means not only is Christ the head of the Church, He dwells there in power. There is *no* power that is greater than Christ's power. His power is greater than the enemy's, but most of all—and this is important to remember—His power is greater than our own. Psalm 33 reminds us: "For he spoke and it came to be; he commanded and it stood firm. The Lord foils the plans of the nations; he thwarts the purposes of the peoples." God is in charge. He is over all and in all and through all. No one has more power than Him.

If no power is greater than the power of God, and that power is unleashed in your life and in your church, imagine the possibilities! Lives will be changed. Conversions and baptisms will take place. People will be called into ministry. Emotional, spiritual and physical healing will take place. The church will grow. It's the most natural thing in the world. Christ is supreme and therefore when His power dwells among us and in us, true spiritual transformation takes place. The Body starts to get well.

Clearly, we need to find and yield to God's power. We should be those who find out where that power is at work and then do all we can to augment it and support it. Instead of viewing the church as a place to gain personal power, as many do, we should be about offering our lives to the power of God at work in the church. Gratefully, the church is never going to be in a position where it will lose power because its head is Christ and He is supreme. The church has all the power it needs because of a direct connection to the power source. Our challenge is to tap into that power instead of depending on our own.

Not only is the power of Christ supreme, it is also sufficient. Contrary to the voices of our culture, you do not need anything else in your life other than Christ. Paul writes in Colossians 1:19-20, "All the fullness of God dwells in Christ and through Him all things are reconciled." With Christ as our head, we can be assured that He is not going to hold anything back from us. Nothing is going to be hidden. God will never fail to provide for us what is needed. All the *fullness* of God dwells in Christ. The fullness of God. It's not the "partial" nature of God. It's the fullness of God. The fullness of God dwells in Christ, and Christ dwells in us. Thus the power of God in Christ is sufficient for *all* our needs.

One of the more memorable advertising campaigns of the past few years is for AFLAC supplemental health insurance. Who can forget that duck that keeps yelling "AFLAC"? The duck keeps trying, but no one seems to be listening. The take-away is clear: your current insurance coverage is not enough. It may cover *some* things, but it won't cover *everything*. It is insufficient. Thus, you need supplemental health insurance. Well, guess what? The world is trying to convince us of the same thing.

We are getting told by the false teachers of our day that Jesus Christ is a fine, wonderful example of a well-lived human life, but He's not enough. We need to supplement our faith with an understanding of how the culture has changed. We need to supplement our faith with a broader, more inclusive moral view of the world. We are certainly free to follow the teachings of Christ, but we need to allow other truths to supplement the truth of Jesus. Jesus is not sufficient. We need something else. Wrong.

Just as Ephaphras taught the Colossians, Christ is all we need. Who shall supply all our needs? Christ! Who is strong when I am weak? Christ! Who has made me rich by His poverty? Christ! Who will never leave me or forsake me? Christ! And it is this Christ—the all-powerful, all-sufficient Christ—who is the Head of the Church. Powerful. Supreme. Sufficient.

Power Outage?

While the all-powerful argument sounds good in theory, it still falls flat for many. If God is all-powerful, why is the Church struggling so mightily in our country? Why do so many who claim the name of Christ seem to live in the absence of spiritual joy and abundance? How is it that Christian faith has come to be viewed as an irrelevant institution out of sync with modern culture? With these questions in play, do we leap to the conclusion that what has been said here is false? Do we surmise that while Christ was powerful at one time, He is impotent now? I think not.

We would be wise to revisit Paul's words. In Colossians 2:18, Paul writes:

> "Do not let anyone who delights in false humility…disqualify you for the prize. Such a person goes into great detail about what he has seen, and his unspiritual mind

puffs him up with idle notions. He has lost connection with the Head, from whom the whole Body, supported and held together by its ligaments and sinews, grows as God causes it to grow."

Is it Christ who has become impotent? Is it Christ who has lost His sufficiency? No. We have lost the transforming power of God and our relevance to a dark world because we have become disconnected from the head, Jesus Christ. We have become detached from the source of our power and sufficiency. Naturally, the more we become disconnected from the headship of Christ, the more our lives and our message become weak and irrelevant.

I am no scientist, but I did a little research on the nature of the human body. When you look at the functions of the human brain, they are staggering. Each part is responsible for some major area—feelings or speech or motor skills. The cerebrum controls most of your body parts and vital organs. The cerebellum controls all muscular activity—arms and legs and balance and basic movement. The medulla controls all of your involuntary responses like blinking, sneezing, coughing and breathing. When all of these signals are firing correctly, the body is a finely tuned machine moving fluidly and gracefully through life. However, it only works when the body is *connected* to the *head*. If the brain gets cut off from one part of the body, that part of the body weakens and eventually ceases to function.

It is the same in our relationship with God. He is the head, and as long as we are connected to Him—submitting to Him, living under His authority, guided by His wisdom—then we have the power to move and live and serve; we have the sufficiency of the One who can meet all our needs. We are connected. However, when we make a choice to follow false teachers, pursue false doctrines, carelessly handle truth or live according to our own desires, we can expect impotence. When we approach our relationship with God only as a casual afterthought or when we allow ourselves to be disconnected from the One who is the Head, then what can we expect will happen? Impotence. Apathetic, meaningless living. Powerless ministry. We can fully expect that absolutely *nothing* will happen.

In a 2002 sermon at Parkside Church in Cleveland, Alistair Begg, read from a speech John Stott gave to the leaders of the Anglican Church. He quoted Stott as saying:

> "It is very easy to see why the church is struggling today. Her leaders—her clergy—her elders—her members are failing to relate the Word of God to the world in which they live, failing to study, discarding what they don't want as if they are the arbiters of truth, flagrantly disobeying its ethical standards and moral teaching, and manipulating its meaning to whatever end they so desire. It is no wonder the church is languishing all over the world because its leaders do not bow to the supreme authority and headship of Christ."

If we wonder why we are living in the absence of the supreme and sufficient power of God, here's why: we are not bowing to the headship of Christ. We have become disconnected from the One who is the true and only leader. We've allowed ourselves to slide down the slippery slope Paul warned us about in Colossians 2:8: "See to it that no one takes you captive through hollow and deceptive philosophy...." Very subtly and very gradually, many who claim the name of Christ have found themselves captured, and having been captured, they become disconnected.

What's the Answer?
Perhaps that is the place where you find yourself today. Disconnected. Powerless. Drowning. You have allowed the world to influence your choices and decisions and as a result, you are feeling dark and hopeless. If we are disconnected, how do we become engaged and reconnect? At some point, I believe all of us will ask that question. I know I have.

When I accepted my first call to pastor a church, I found myself in the midst of a community that, for many reasons, was wounded, insecure and lacking any kind of theological or biblical identity. Members bickered among themselves, rehashing the past while harshly criticizing anything I did to help them move forward in a new direction. It felt dead and lifeless. Ministry became a labor. In a rare communication with one of my theological heroes, I asked John Stott, "What is the key to renewing a dead or broken church?" I assumed that his answer would be something like, "You need to be more committed to prayer" or "You need to improve your worship." It was neither.

Instead he told me the key to renewing a dead or broken church—or a spiritually dead or broken person—is "the faithful proclamation and teaching of the Word of God." In other words, renewal comes when you reconnect to the power of what is true. You must reconnect to the prescription offered by the Healer. By being in the Word, we reconnect the body to the head. We go right back to Colossians 2:18. When the body is connected to the head, what happens? The body grows. It is happening all over the world in churches that honor and lift up the name of Christ and stand beneath the authority of His Word. Growth—staggering, wonderful growth. Korea, Africa and home churches in China are just a few examples. The Church is finding renewal and true transforming, spiritual power because they understand and are focused on who is in charge. Christ! Christ is the head of their churches and they are bowing before His authority.

In the same way, I have found that those who come into my office sagging from the weight of their choices find relief when they are nurtured and fed by the Word of God. Our spiritual health and vitality depends on us being centered in Christ and submitting ourselves to His headship. Of course, that is much easier said than done.

Spiritual health is achieved when we seek to connect our lives and submit our lives to the One who is the head—Christ. Why do you think it is important that we worship? We worship so that we connect to Christ. Why is it important that we have opportunities for Bible study, Sunday School, small groups, prayer, and other forms of community? We commit to those endeavors so that we connect to Christ. Why do we invest resources and give money for evangelism and missions? So that others can connect to Christ. Sometimes I think we make our relationship with God too hard. Yes, it is mysterious and deep in many respects. No, we will not fully grasp it on this side of heaven. However, our ability to grow and mature in faith—our ability to experience more of what God has for us—is not complicated. Connect to the head. Bow to His authority. Submit to His Word. Then, stand back. Powerful things will happen. Peace and security will be born in our midst by His sufficiency. Lives will be transformed.

Are We Listening?

I don't do a lot of flying, but I have noticed something interesting when I get on an airplane. About the time that you have settled into your seat and put your things away, the flight attendants begin a demonstration. Either in-person or by video, they present all the information that you need to know in order to survive in an emergency. They show you how to buckle your seat belt, put on an oxygen mask, use your seat cushion as a floatation device, and find the exits. This is all well and good, except that no one listens! Most people on the plane are completely disconnected from the presentation which is provided to help save their lives! Instead, they clack away at their computers or iPhones, oblivious to the life-saving message being shared.

I think many of us may be living our lives like those "checked out" airline passengers. We may be on board, but we are not connected to the important, life-saving information. The information we need to save our lives is easily accessible, but in our smug confidence, we are apathetic and convinced of our self-sufficiency.

My prayer is that the power of Christ—the sufficiency of Christ—will be plainly evident to you because you understand one thing: there's only one person who is in charge. A serious problem exists, but thankfully, there is someone who knows what to do. There's one person who has the remedy. It's not David Swanson. It's not you. It's not John Stott or any other Christian leader. It is Christ. You are being called—by the Creator of the universe—to be vital, healthy and alive so that you may be empowered to become the person God intended you to be and experience the full abundance of His love. Only as we yield to His headship, the one who is in charge, will we experience that abundance.

Part Two

IDENTIFYING THE VITAL SIGNS

4

"All this shows us that the real crisis over worship, in the history of the church and perhaps especially today, is this: will God's people wake up to worshiping God in such a way that we demonstrate we are awake by loving our neighbor in God's name?"

MARK LABERTON, THE DANGEROUS ACT OF WORSHIP

"They broke bread in their homes and ate together with glad and sincere hearts, praising God and enjoying the favor of all the people. And the Lord added to their number daily those who were being saved."

ACTS 2:46-47

Last summer, during a much needed vacation, I came across a book by Dallas Willard called *The Great Omission*. I had been trying to make sense of an apparent lack of vitality among those who profess Christian faith and it seemed Willard was writing directly to me:

> *"There is an obvious great disparity between, on the one hand, the hope for life expressed in Jesus—found real in the Bible and in many shining examples from among his followers—and, on the other hand, the actual day-to-day behavior, inner life, and social presence of most of those who now profess adherence to him. The question must arise: Why the great disparity?"*

Why, indeed. We know what the problem is and we know who has the solution, but still we struggle to live out of the faith which we express. Willard's answer relates to discipleship, and while that's certainly part of the answer, it's not the whole answer. I believe it goes beyond that.

If we are to experience the "hope for life expressed in Jesus," how will our lives need to be reshaped? What will allow us to grow in Christ more deeply and live out our faith more freely? These questions will shape the next portion of this book, and I hope that by applying what you read, you can build a relationship with God that is more than something you merely ascribe to, but something that is dynamically occurring in you and through you.

In the Presence of Power

During the fall of 2003, my wife and I had a "once in a lifetime" experience that will forever remain etched in our memories. A dear friend in Ft. Myers invited us to attend a fundraiser for President George W. Bush. At the time, the President was campaigning for re-election and this event was part of his Florida tour. Naturally, we were elated. Regardless of your political affiliations, the opportunity to meet a sitting President doesn't present itself every day.

As the event drew near, Leigh and I found ourselves becoming obsessed. We couldn't stop talking about what it would be like, what we would say to the President, who we might see—it was ridiculous! I think my biggest fear was that I would say something stupid to the most powerful man in the free world. "Hello, Mr. President. Sorry about those weapons of mass destruction." You get the point. The big day finally arrived, and though it was a dinner, not scheduled to begin until 5 p.m., we both woke up earlier than normal.

I'm not the kind of guy that thinks much about what to wear, but that morning I found myself paralyzed, standing before my closet. Red tie or yellow? Grey suit or blue? Which belt? Do I have clean socks? If I was struggling that much over *my* clothing choices, you can only imagine how my wife was faring. I'm pretty sure she enlisted the help of what seemed like 24 girlfriends, and still she tried on her entire closet that morning.

Finally, wardrobe selections were put to rest; however, our jitters were not. We left the house over an hour early for a short, 15 minute drive. When we arrived—early, no doubt—and made our way toward a large tent set-up on the lawn, we couldn't help but notice there was security absolutely everywhere we looked; secret service agents disguised as gardeners (most gardeners don't wear earpieces and black dress shoes), huge muscle-bound men dressed in all black, police boats on the river, helicopters overhead, and even armed divers who popped up out of the water. Never have I felt so safe and secure!

Once we finally reached the seating area, we were stunned to discover we were seated in the front row, only about 20 feet from the podium, where the President would address the crowd. And sure enough, when he concluded his remarks and stepped down to greet the audience, he walked right toward us! I speak in front of a crowd for a living. I can assure you that I am not normally at a loss for words, and yet in that moment, my palms were sweaty, my stomach was in knots, and my heart was racing as I struggled with what to say.

At last, there he was before me, and I introduced myself. He could not have been nicer. Leigh and I spoke of our roots in Texas, our devotion to his former team, the Texas Rangers, and our role in ministry in the church. He asked us questions about our church and our home, and expressed his appreciation for our prayers. It was truly an exciting moment.

Later that night, as we relived every last detail, I found myself thinking about the invitation we receive every day to worship the living God. No question, it was thrilling and an honor to meet the President of the United States, yet, other than his role in government, what had he done for us personally that had changed or enriched our lives? I suppose you could make a case for something related to national security or some program that I have benefitted from. I don't doubt that. Even so, I was dumbstruck by the lack of significance I assign to my standing invitation to dwell in the presence of the Living God.

Why don't we treat God's daily invitation with the same anticipation and reverence as we do some earthly ones? I don't know about you, but I don't linger in my closet thinking about what I will wear on Sunday morning. I would bet you don't arrive at your church an hour early just to be sure you don't miss anything. I doubt you spend days speculating what the sermon will be about or laboring over just exactly what to say in your prayers. I'm pretty sure you don't find your heart racing or your palms sweating at the mere thought of being in God's presence. It's kind of a shame that we don't.

Why do most people leap at the prospect of meeting powerful, influential men and women, yet dismiss the privilege of meeting with the God of heaven and earth, as if it were of no significance? I think the answer is because we have lost our perspective on what worship is all about—on what is truly happening, spiritually, when we enter the sanctuary of God. (By sanctuary, I mean any place—outside or inside—where the people of God gather to worship. It is not defined merely as a physical edifice.)

If we are to live vital, healthy, Christian lives, we must understand the heart of worship, and in so doing, reclaim our ability to truly worship. Do you ever notice that Christians like to talk about prayer more than they like to actually pray? We like to talk about worship more than we actually worship. We need to learn how to move beyond the talk.

Vital Sign #1: Worship

One attribute of a vital, healthy Christian (or a vital, healthy church) is a deep love for and understanding of worship. It is what marked the growing, vital church of the New Testament as the young saints of God began to order their lives together. In the second chapter of Acts, Luke makes it clear that worship was at the core of everything the church did. He goes on to describe the miraculous birth of the church, the pouring out of the Holy Spirit, the gifts that came upon God's people, and the ensuing flood of converts who—having been touched by the grace of God in Jesus Christ—swarmed the church. Luke details the Holy Spirit's effect on the people. They began to live and act in a way that made their body healthy. And the most important of those new behaviors was *worship*. Acts 2:42, 46 says:

> *"They devoted themselves to the Apostles teaching and to the fellowship, to the breaking of bread and to prayer. They broke bread together with glad and sincere hearts, praising God and enjoying the favor of all the people."*

You could argue that "devotion to teaching" was related to discipleship and Bible study, but the other four elements—fellowship, breaking bread, prayer and praise—were all about worship. Sacramental, consistent, community worship. If the early church was healthy and growing, and worship was central to their community, what can we learn from them to help improve our understanding and practice of worship?

Before we do that, let's step back and answer a more fundamental question: why worship? Some people worship out of a sense of duty or obligation. It's what they are supposed to do. Others worship because they like the feeling of being with others. They get to see friends and be with family. They feel cared for. Others worship without really knowing why, simply hoping to connect with something bigger than themselves. Still others only attend worship, never actually worshipping, because they have been dragged there by someone else. In the pantheon of reasons to worship, there is often precious little attention given to the object of our worship: God. Sometimes, the last reason we go to worship is to actually worship.

If that's the case, then of course worship is meaningless. We've lost our inspiration. We don't understand the object of our worship, therefore our worship is bland and dull. True worship is inspired by a clear recognition of the wonder and awe of the person being worshipped. Luke writes in Acts 2:43, "Everyone was filled with awe." The people who surrounded Jesus and heard him speak and watched him serve were inspired. The text goes on to mention the "wonders and miraculous signs" performed by the apostles in God's name. What they observed created awe. They were awestruck by the incarnate Son of God, Jesus Christ and therefore, they *worshipped*.

Think for a moment about what was happening. God was on the move. Lives were being changed. People were being healed. The Gospel was being preached. The Spirit was at work. God was present in a palpable, transforming way, and the people were awestruck. When you are awestruck, it is hard not to worship. God is great! God is glorious! God is faithful!

When I compare the early church to Christians today, I find this understanding of God's nature to be the critical element. It explains our apathy and our struggle to truly understand and live into worship as God intended. Our worship will never be more than a trifling, perfunctory duty unless we truly discover—and internalize—the glory and wonder of God. Period. If you are not awestruck by the incarnation, speechless that God would die for you, touched that God has forgiven you, and moved by the glory that awaits you, then you will never experience true worship. In our culture, it is particularly hard to remember and internalize the fact that worship is not about us. Worship is about God. Without understanding that, there is no inspiration.

I play basketball every week. I'm committed and I give it my all, but no one comes to see me play and no one asks for my autograph. I just don't inspire much of a following. However, anytime LeBron James or Kobe Bryant step onto a court, they attract huge crowds. People wait in line for hours for an autograph, or just a glimpse, of these men. The real difference, of course, is my game inspires *no one*. To watch LeBron or Kobe is to watch a superhuman superhero, and it is inspiring. People are awestruck by their physical gifts to play basketball. My point is that we "worship" those who inspire awe. We worship those we believe have something worthy of our praise.

It is no different in our spiritual lives. If you are not inspired by the wonder of God, your worship will always be empty. However, when the Holy Spirit touches your heart and brings the truth of God's nature to life—when you pursue God not for His benefits, but because you love Him—then worship becomes powerful and transformational. Worship becomes central to your life. It will be an indispensable part of your existence because you have seen the wonder of God and you yearn to express the sense of awe and wonder that you feel.

In Acts 2, worship is associated with both reverence and gladness or joy. Acts 2:46 says, "They broke bread in their homes and ate together with glad and sincere hearts, praising God and enjoying the favor of all the people." There was a deep sense of reverence for the wonder and holiness of God. However, that reverence did not diminish the joy and gladness they felt towards God. They were not so awestruck as to be unable to speak or stand. Even in their awe, they were inspired to express themselves through worship. Their hearts were free to worship and praise God in a manner that was honest and heartfelt.

To be clear, I'm a Presbyterian. We Presbyterians struggle a bit with this idea. Yes, we want to be reverent, but sometimes our reverence becomes so consuming that our worship has no joy. We stand and sit and sing and pray in an almost endless monotone of joylessness.

I've been to some churches that make you feel like you're at a carnival. The environment is so casual, so focused on fun, that even a pastor in a top hat introducing a three-ring circus wouldn't surprise anyone. There is no reverence. Clearly, the answer has to be somewhere in the middle of these two extremes. We should reverently bow before the Almighty, but we should do so with gladness and joy. Like many facets of our relationship with God, we must learn to hold these two dynamics in tension.

On the one hand, we know God is holy and glorious. We know that were we to encounter the fullness of His glory, we would perish. We simply could not bear it. On the other hand, we know that He wants our worship. He wants us to seek His presence. Thus, worship should humble you and it should move you. Not because worship is about you, but because God's presence is humbling and moving. You should sense, almost in the same moment, the utter holiness of God and the tender touch of His hand. You cannot let go of either dynamic or your worship becomes compromised. If you let go of His glory, your worship will never be inspired, but if you let go of His tenderness, you'll only be able to shudder in fear.

As a pastor, I have no desire to lead a circus. Worship is reverent and ordered because of the nature of the God we worship. He is not chaotic. He is ordered. I also have no desire to lead people who have no joy or gladness at the invitation to be in God's presence. It has to be both. Sadly, it is this tension that has created conflict over worship as Christians, in so many churches, argue about which dynamic to emphasize and how.

Togetherness
This tension brings me to my second point: worship is to be experienced *together*. Many of the words used to describe the early church in Acts 2 are words in the plural, implying that the church was always doing things together. They were functioning and ministering in groups, not in isolation. They met—together. They ate—together. They served—together. They praised—together. To that end, those who know and trust in God, and are awestruck by His wonder and grace, are called to worship—together.

It is not my intention to diminish in any way the daily, individual moments in which people worship God. Even so,

God's clear call is for us to be together as one body, celebrating, praying, and experiencing community. In John 17, Jesus prays that we might be "one" as He was one with the Father. He emphasizes that the unity of the body becomes a witness to the world. I believe the primary means by which we grow in unity is through worship.

When we worship together, we are led to common ground. There is no hierarchy. There are no positions. There are no groups or clubs. In most worship services, you begin with some element of praise and adoration to God. You become aware of who God is—His wonder and holiness. You start to have that sense of awe. Naturally, when you realize who God is, you become acutely aware of who you are. By comparison, you are nothing. You are flawed in every conceivable way. You are darkened by sin. It should then become quite apparent that you are in need of God's grace; which is why praise is often followed by confessional prayer. And that's where you find the common ground.

We are all in the same boat, flawed and undeserving, in need of God's grace. All of us are broken. All of us are on equal footing with every other human being in the world, but especially those with whom we worship. It's a bit like an Alcoholics Anonymous meeting. AA has had great success in helping people battle addiction because they get people on common ground. It does not matter who you are outside the meeting. "Hello, my name is Joe, and I'm an alcoholic." In such meetings, there are no bankers or schoolteachers, electricians or coaches. No, everyone is an alcoholic, and the recognition of that common ground is what unites them.

The same is true for the Christian community. We might do well to stand up in church and say, "Hello, my name is Joe, and I'm a sinner. I need God's grace." That's the posture we assume, or should assume, in worship. In Christian worship, no one is greater and no one is lesser. We all stand before God in need of the cleansing blood of Jesus Christ and the renewing grace of His Holy Spirit. In worship we find our common ground. Therefore, if a body does not worship, or if individuals subtract themselves from worship, there can be no unity. Without unity, our ministry and witness in the world are diminished.

Not long ago, I ran into a couple from church who had been regular attenders, but whom I hadn't seen in awhile.

They hadn't agreed with some decisions that were made in a particular ministry, and as a result, quit coming to our church. When I asked where they were attending now, he said, "We just worship at home. It's been great. We sing some songs as a family. I read the Scripture and give a devotional. For now, it's really working."

While I didn't say it, I thought it was sad. Here was a member of the body, and because he was disturbed by an imperfection in the body, he withdrew. I have noticed this is a recurring phenomenon: we act surprised when a body of sinful and flawed people do things that are sinful and flawed. There's an old saying that goes, "If you ever find a perfect church, don't join it. You'll ruin it." The fact is the Christian community is made up of people just like you and me. It's not perfect. Even so, it seems that when a church encounters struggles, worship is the first thing to go. The thing that is supposed to be the foundation of our unity is used to manipulate and punish.

"Pastor Joe isn't doing things the way I want, so I'm not going to church."

"I can't believe I wasn't asked to be on that committee. I'm not going to participate at all."

"Sally said something rude to me last week. I don't want to run into her—I'm not going to go to church."

"This denomination is ridiculous. I'm so tired of the politics. We need to go somewhere else."

"I don't like the way they're spending our money. I'm not going anymore."

We tend to express our pleasure or displeasure with certain elements of church life by our participation (or lack thereof) in worship. Worship should not be hijacked for any other purpose than to ascribe glory to God! Worship should be motivated and inspired solely by the wonder of God. He alone is worthy to receive it. It should not be driven by external circumstances which may surround the body at any given time.

The common bond of our need for grace and forgiveness is far greater than anything that might divide us. You may not like every one or agree with every one, but if their faith is as genuine as yours, you will live with them in eternity. If you are going to live with them in eternity, shouldn't you find a way to live with them here, too? Our commitment to the body should never be so self-serving that a change in the circumstances of that body would lead us away from worship. I would hope and pray that our perspective on worship is grounded in the nature and character of God—the awe and wonder He inspires—and not the nature and character of our neighbors or the nature of the circumstances we currently face. Worship should draw us together, not pull us apart.

Worship Wars

In the church today, I am not sure that anything has the power to pull us apart more than the form of our worship. Someone coined the phrase "worship wars" to describe this unfortunate phenomenon. Even so, I was confident that I knew enough about worship and church leadership that such a thing would never play out in a church where I was pastor. Wrong. Three years ago, our church decided to rearrange the timing and format of our Sunday worship schedule. I wanted our services to be more available to the un-churched, so believing that group would more likely attend at a later hour, we moved our non-traditional, seeker service into our sanctuary at 11 a.m. and moved our traditional service 75 minutes earlier to 9:45 a.m. I assumed everyone would see my logic and enthusiastically support my vision for this new outreach. Not hardly. A few minor changes created a whole lot of conflict. Attendance dropped. Giving dropped. The pervasive conversation among our body turned from God's work in our ministry to the "worship controversy." It dominated everything we did.

Stubbornly, I didn't want to change anything. I kept thinking people would catch on, but they didn't. Finally, after ten months of decline, I backtracked. I moved the traditional service back into the sanctuary at 11 a.m. and the seeker service out of the sanctuary into our Fellowship Hall. Almost immediately, the conflict disappeared. When people got what they wanted in regard to their preferred worship style and time, they acted as if nothing ever happened.

It was quite the learning experience. I learned that the church has become so adept at separating people into age groups and worship categories that we scarcely know one another. We lack the unity Christ prays for because we have no sense of what it means to worship together. We are not one body, but many bodies. Children do one thing, escorted out of the service, much to the delight of frantic parents. Students have their own youth-centric programs. We have a group for those who are divorced, a group for singles in their 20s and couples in their 30s. We have a group for left-handed men and a group for women over six-feet tall. Not really, but I hope you see my point. We are separated, and that affects our ability to worship as a community.

Once again, we need to accept that at the foot of the cross, before a glorious and gracious God, we share common ground that trumps any earthly barrier that might otherwise separate us. Even so, among the body, there are varying opinions, tastes and preferences. We want to be accommodating, so we offer these different forms. However, I have to believe that the bond we share in Jesus Christ is more important than any age affinity or musical preference. While I understand the need for different forms of worship, if we have them, we have to be all the more diligent about creating other avenues for uniting the body.

God calls us to worship together because it is in that community that barriers are broken down. I think we make a huge mistake by segregating 17-year-olds from 70-year-olds when the truth is, through faith, what they have in common supersedes different taste in music. Worship should be blind to race and age and gender and socio-economic status. I'm not saying we can't offer different forms of worship. I am saying we need to be sensitive about how those forms are presented and what impact those forms have on the church body as a whole. It is a very difficult dynamic.

One of my favorite presentations of the Gospel in a mainstream movie is from *Places in the Heart*, for which Sally Field won a Best Actress Oscar in 1984. The movie, also starring Danny Glover and John Malkovich, explores the relational struggles of a family in the rural Midwest as they cope with infidelity, racism, classism, divorce, violence and even tornados. In one climactic scene, a drunken white man accidentally shoots and kills a young black boy. It is a sad and poignant scene, which crystallizes the underlying emotions of both the characters and the audience.

As the movie draws to a close, the characters are in church, singing hymns with contented, peaceful smiles on their faces. As the service progresses, communion is served and the camera closes in on the main characters as they receive the sacrament, and then gradually, the camera pulls back. As it does,

all the characters in the film are revealed, even those who
have died. The betrayed wife passes the communion plate
to her unfaithful husband. The mistreated, black field hand
passes the plate to the bigoted, white landowner. Finally, the
young black boy passes the plate to the drunken white man
who killed him, and suddenly you realize you are not looking
at an earthly scene, but a heavenly one; the holy ground at
the foot of the cross, a place of worship where, in the end, all
those who live by faith are one.

It is as the Church should be. It is the perspective that we
should have as we enter into worship, but sadly, our sin often
gets in the way. Yes, we worship on this side of heaven, but we
do so with the understanding that our worship today is but a
rehearsal for what will come later. We are bound together in
Christ by faith. We are graciously loved and forgiven, and the
grace of God that we receive unites us in the most glorious
manner as we worship together. *Together.*

Vertical, Not Horizontal

Finally, it is important that our worship maintain a proper
sense of direction. It is a personal act of praise, offered most
commonly in the community of faith, directed towards God. It
is vertical, not horizontal. Living in the world we do, it is easy
to lose sight of this. We live in an entertainment-saturated society. Everything about our world is driven by who can enter-
tain us and who can keep our attention. We are quite familiar
with the model by which we are entertained: we go to a large
venue with a large number of other people. We sit in seats
placed side by side, all facing a stage. Once there, we watch as
someone performs for us and we express our pleasure, or lack
thereof, by our applause. Our only job is to sit back and enjoy
what is happening up front. We are the audience. Everything
is done for us. It is a horizontal experience. This explains why
our worship has become directionally challenged. We walk
into a sanctuary or worship space and we see a large room
with a lot of other people, all seated and facing what looks
like a stage. We interpret those on the "stage" to be the per-
formers. We assume our job is to receive. We get lulled into
believing we are spectators, rather than participants.

This is not a model of Biblical worship. When you go to
worship, you are not part of an audience. God is the audience.
You are not receiving, you are giving. You are a participant.

You are the one doing the act of worship. Psalm 103 says, "Bless the Lord, O my soul, and all that is within me bless His holy name." David is the one engaged in worship. David is the one blessing the name of the Lord. The direction is vertical, not horizontal. The role of the worship leader is to help you make an offering to the Lord, but their actions are not directed toward you. Their actions are intended to lead you toward the vertical dynamic of what is happening between you and the Lord. Thus, rather than critiquing the choir or the band, maybe you should be asking yourself, "Did I bring an acceptable sacrifice of worship to the Lord?" It is why we sing and pray and praise and testify and proclaim the Word—that what we do might be our gift to God.

Now, to be sure, when you worship, you get something. You are blessed. You are blessed because as you worship, the presence of God comes down. Psalm 22:3 tells us that, "God inhabits the praise of His people." When we worship, God comes down and is present. When He is present, what happens? Lives change. Hearts melt. Attitudes improve. Perspectives shift.

In Acts 2:47, because they were faithful in worship, God was "adding to their number daily." When you come to offer God the gift of your worship, He winds up meeting you and blessing you. When the church worships together in a healthy way, God moves. People come to faith. People encounter God. People's hearts are moved and changed by God. It is for that reason that from time to time, after worship, I give an invitation for anyone who would like to receive Christ, rededicate their life to Christ or respond to His leading in some way. I do this because when we worship, God is at work. Hearts get touched. I am convinced that when we begin to worship in a holy way as a body, the church grows beyond our expectations and imagination.

More Than a Pacifier

When our kids were little, each one of them developed an affinity for a little device that Leigh and I came to consider a life-saver: the pacifier. For children, a pacifier is used to quell desire. They're hungry—or upset—and what they want is the comfort of their mother's breast, but instead, they get a cold, plastic substitute. Amazingly, we found the pacifier worked most of the time. We found that we could often get them to focus on the pacifier and, in doing so, deflect their hunger or calm their fears. However, it only worked for a time. Eventually, their hunger or their fears would become so strong that nothing would suffice other than the arms of Mom or Dad. It is how God made us.

As a child of God, we are made for communion with the Father. Naturally, we hunger for Him—to be in His presence. You and I are made for worship. Sometimes we don't understand that and we use "pacifiers" to deflect the true hunger of our hearts—cheap, cold, plastic worldly substitutes. Eventually, though, our hearts will be quiet no longer. Eventually, the true hunger of our hearts will lead us to worship, to the wonder and majesty and mystery of God; to the presence of our Christian brothers and sisters and to the powerful movement of God's Holy Spirit in our lives as we offer ourselves to Him. A vital sign of a healthy Christian life, or a healthy Christian body, is one that hungers and thirsts for the real thing—for God—through worship.

5 ✓

A HEART THAT GROWS:
WORSHIP AS TRANSFORMATION

"Mom, can I have some spinach?"

ALEX SWANSON, AGE 4, AFTER WATCHING
AN EPISODE OF POPEYE THE SAILORMAN

*"About midnight, Paul and Silas were praying
and singing hymns to God, and the other prisoners were listening."*

ACTS 16:25

I have three children: John David is 18 and, at the time of this writing, about to graduate from high school. Alex is 17 and a junior. Kaylee is 15 and a freshman. I am deeply grateful to God for each of them and for the season we are in now. Not only do we love our children, but we enjoy them as well. We love spending time with them. Not only that, but my children have been the Lord's constant instruments in my life. Throughout their lives, often unbeknownst to them, they have been God's messengers to me. Sometimes they teach me about the world, sometimes they teach me about myself, and sometimes they just test my patience! When Alex, my middle child, was four, he had what I imagine is a typical little boy fascination with superheroes—capes, flying, the whole deal. Of course, this obsession quickly turned to frustration when he realized, despite his best efforts, he could not fly. No matter how many times he stretched out his arms and authoritatively proclaimed, "Up, up and away!" nothing happened. He found this very distressing.

Like many boys, he had a set of Superman pajamas that he wore around the house almost constantly. One afternoon, I came home from work early, and sure enough, Alex was "flying" around the house in his Superman jammies. I didn't think twice about it. This was typical early evening fare. I sat down at the kitchen table to look at the mail, not really paying attention to Alex's flight path. Without me realizing it, Alex went out on the back deck, climbed up on the picnic table and then hoisted himself onto the railing on the top of our deck. (I know. You are thinking I am a lousy, inattentive father!) Before I realized what was happening, he made eye contact with me, shouted, "Up, up and away!" and leaped off the deck, arms outstretched. The ground beneath him was grassy, but it was still a one-story drop. Terrified, I ran out to the yard and found him, bloody lip and all, smiling about his journey to the ground, still mad that it had not lasted longer. There were tears, but mostly he wanted to know, "Daddy, did you see me fly?"

The next day, feeling as though we needed to broaden Alex's horizons, Leigh pulled out some old Popeye videos. They were wholly new to Alex. He had never seen these, and he was engrossed. After watching Popeye do superhuman feats (all without leaving the ground!) following the ingestion of spinach, you could almost see the wheels turning in his little head.

"Mom, can I have some spinach?" he asked. He had witnessed something amazing and was sure the key to this miracle was within his reach. So naturally, he thought, "I need to get some of that!" When it comes to how we understand worship as a part of our relationship with God, I think this is often exactly how it works. We all have a desire to fly, to soar through life experiencing the abundance and joy promised us by God, yet we don't. We find ourselves hungry and searching until, that is, we see someone else experiencing what we want. We see someone in the presence of God, worshipping with a deep sense of God's love and power, and our hearts cry out, "Can I please have some of that?"

At its core, Christian worship, in any form, should be something that ignites desire and envy in others. Our worship should be attractive and powerful to the world. It should be a witness. Every human being longs for something which, in many respects, they cannot articulate. C.S. Lewis speaks to this concept in his famous sermon, *The Weight of Glory*:

> *"The inconsolable secret in every one of us…is a longing to be reunited with something in the universe from which we all now feel cut off the longing to be on the inside of some door which we have always seen from the outside—that longing—that inconsolable longing—that secret—is no mere neurotic fantasy—but it's the truest index of our real*

situation. The sense that in this universe we are strang-
ers—the longing to be acknowledged—to meet with some
response—to bridge some chasm that yawns between us
and reality is part of our inconsolable secret..."

We yearn for peace and meaning and hope, but cannot find the key that unlocks the door. If worship unlocks the door, as it should, then when others see us in that experience, it should compel them to say, "I want that too! That's what I'm missing!" Instead, there is nothing to see but a lack of enthusiasm, a lack of power, a lack of interest, a lack of pretty much anything other than apathy. If worship is not changing us, why should we expect anyone else to be interested? If we are to grow into the people that God desires for us to be—healthy and vital and alive—then our worship must be compelling and vital. Healthy Christians and healthy churches worship with spirit and passion and genuine awe. In which case, is our lack of healthy Christian living a result of our lack of vital worship or vice versa?

Gotta Have It
Generally speaking, some of my favorite hours of the day come between 11 p.m. and 6 a.m.—namely, the hours I am sleeping. I love to sleep and I am still fairly good at it. I don't have any trouble falling asleep and most of the time, I stay asleep through the night. I love to make the house cold, pull up the blankets and snooze. It's wonderful.

Five years ago, however, I had a rather unusual night. We had only been living in Orlando a short time, my new position at First Presbyterian Church was fairly consuming (OK— very consuming), and I was facing some problems for which there were no easy answers. I had just moved my children from a city where they were happy to a city where they had no friends. They were struggling as was my wife.

At church, I felt pressure to get off to a strong start so the congregation would be confident I was the right choice. There was financial pressure, as the two homes to which we were contractually engaged—one we were selling and one we were buying—had both been damaged by Hurricane Charlie. I was facing mountains of insurance paperwork and the customary haggling over coverage. Frankly, I was feeling overwhelmed, anxious and discouraged.

One night in the midst of this turmoil, I went to bed at the usual time and fell asleep quickly. However, I woke at 1:30 a.m. somewhat startled and could not get back to sleep. Over the years, I have come to realize that sometimes God wants me awake in the middle of the night to pray or reflect or read. Thus, I went into our den and began to pray. I prayed for my children transitioning into new schools and making new friends, I prayed about the ministry of my church and the many challenges we were facing, I prayed about my parents and my siblings, my wife, and the men in my small group. I covered all the usual suspects, but still I didn't feel any peace in my spirit. I felt tired, almost disturbed. Not knowing what else to do, I mindlessly turned on the television.

What came on surprised me. There was a stadium full of people, singing. Many of them had tears streaming down their faces, and they sang a single line: "Everywhere I go, I see you." The person leading worship was a Christian artist, Michael W. Smith, and the song was a testimony of the people of Israel. Through the wilderness, God's people had learned that God was present. Right there, in my den, the Holy Spirit made this simple truth come alive and something slightly miraculous happened. I began to sing, echoing back the words: "Everywhere I go, I see you. Everywhere I go, I see you." It touched the core of my soul as I realized that my perspective had been warped by my own understanding, and I was failing to see God in the midst of my circumstances. By then, it was 3 a.m. and I was now on the floor of my den, weeping and singing, "Everywhere I go, I see you." The unique stresses and strains of my life at that time did not magically go away, but I can promise you I lived on that single moment of worship for many days afterward. It was a phrase I often repeated, and still think about years later. It was a tall, cold glass of water to a thirsty man, and I am convinced that God woke me that night for a single purpose: that I might have a healing moment of true, authentic, unbridled worship. Through it, He bore witness to my soul of His eternal love and presence.

As I reflect on that moment, I realize the significance of worship in my life. When I worship honestly and freely, it changes me. It does something to my heart. It makes me acutely aware of how desperately I need God. It makes me realize, yet again, that His love and power have been poured out in me. Without it, I am lost. Without it, I am powerless. Without it, I am defeated.

To be clear, I don't worship like that nearly as often as I would like. I know it when it happens, but that kind of spirit-freeing, empowering, heart-releasing worship is not the norm. Can you remember the last time something like that happened for you? When is the last time you sat in a worship service and felt the door of your heart open and the Spirit of God poured in? I go back to Charles Spurgeon from *The Kiss of the Father:*

> *"Some of us know what it is like to be too happy to live. The love of God has been so overpoweringly experienced by us on some occasions that we almost have to ask God to stop the delight because we could endure no more. If God had not shielded His love and glory a bit, we believe we could not have stood it."*

When is the last time you felt that, and I wonder, why do our churches not worship this way more often? Is it because we are part of some denomination or church body that is just not capable of that kind of worship? I don't think so. I think the reason we fail in our attempts at worship is because we do not hunger for the experience nor do we recognize its power. In her book, *Teaching a Stone to Talk*, Annie Dillard writes:

> *"Does anyone have the foggiest idea what sort of power we so blithely invoke? Or, as I suspect, does no one believe a word of it? The churches are like children playing on the floor with their chemistry sets, mixing up a batch of TNT to kill time on a Sunday morning. It is madness to wear ladies' straw hats and velvet hats to church; we should all be wearing crash helmets. Ushers should issue life preservers and signal flares; they should lash us to our pews for the sleeping God we say we worship may wake one day and take offense..."*

When God's people worship, I believe God shows up, I'm just not sure we always recognize it. As we discussed earlier, He inhabits the praise of His people. Perhaps our struggle is that we do not notice Him when He arrives. When Bruce Springsteen's album, *The Rising*, was released shortly after 9/11, a review in *Time* magazine said:

"The songs are sad, but the sadness is almost always matched with optimism, promises of redemption and calls for spiritual arms. There is more rising on The Rising than in a month of church."

When I read that, my heart sank. Is there more life on a rock 'n' roll album than when believers gather before the God of their salvation? I pray that is not the case. We must reclaim the true heart of worship—what God intends for us to experience—so that it becomes not only food for our souls but a witness to the world of God's love and grace. It should make those around us envy what we have!

Worship in the Jail

In thinking about our desire for true worship, I want to focus on one of the most powerful worship texts in all of Scripture. It comes from Acts 16, and the circumstances which surround Paul and Silas are nothing short of overwhelming. Through the words recorded by Luke, God gives instructions as it relates to this idea of worship as witness. The chapter describes the continuing ministry of Paul as he takes the Gospel of Jesus Christ to the Gentiles. It begins with Paul meeting and enlisting Silas in his ministry. Together, they journey to Troas where they meet a wealthy cloth dealer named Lydia, and in verse 14, she is described as a "worshiper." As a result of her worship, God opens her heart and she responds to the message of the Gospel. Through worship, she is converted to faith, baptized, and becomes a disciple of Jesus Christ.

Next, Luke recounts Paul's experience meeting a slave girl—the antithesis of Lydia, both socially and economically—who is possessed by an evil spirit and being exploited by local men for their personal profit. Paul delivers the girl from the evil spirit, but because he has done something that negatively impacts the financial standing of some locals, they trump up charges against him and Silas. Those charges result in one of the most grisly scenes in the New Testament.

Paul and Silas are dragged in front of a crowd, stripped of their clothes and beaten. In verse 23, the text says they were "severely flogged," which, more than likely, meant most of the flesh was torn off their backs. Horrific. When it was finally over, they were taken to the jail, to an inner cell, where their hands and feet were forced into stocks. This kind of restraint would force their bodies to cramp after only a few minutes. Their backs were bleeding and raw. They were in a lifeless, cold cell. It is difficult to imagine the physical suffering these men endured. When I think about myself in such a situation, I'm pretty sure I would be doing nothing to honor the Lord at that point. I would have likely responded in a way that reflected my despondence over the grim nature of the situation; I would have curled up in a ball and quit or at the very least, used offensive, angry language.

Paul and Silas react in quite the opposite manner. Acts 16:25 says, "About midnight, Paul and Silas were praying and singing hymns to God, and the other prisoners were listening." I find this response one of the most stunning testimonies in all of Scripture. Given their circumstances, I am awestruck by their worship. It's almost surreal. I cannot fathom it. It is a moment rich with truth about worship and I want to look at two things that I hope will be instructive as you think and reflect on this text.

First, while it seems inconceivable to us, we need to understand how it was possible for Paul and Silas to react in this way. Look at the context. Paul and Silas were engaged in ministry—serving the Lord—and they could *see* His power at work. They could see His movement. Lydia comes to worship and she is changed. She encountered the living God and her life was transformed. The slave girl encountered the power of Christ and was delivered from an evil spirit. Right before their eyes, God tangibly demonstrated that there is no greater power than the power of the living God. Yes, Paul and Silas wind up in jail, but I believe it was in jail that they had the time and space to reflect on all that had taken place. I believe they realized that God was both the God of the mountain as well as the God of the valley. Paul and Silas were under no delusion that faith and service would result in only circumstantial blessings. They knew that sometimes, God would allow hard things—challenging circumstances—into their lives. Even so, He was still God; that was never in question. Despite personal hardships and difficulties, Paul and Silas still believed wholeheartedly that God loved them and was still at work. Even in jail, they did what they knew would encourage them. They did what they could to lift up their hearts. They did their best to bear witness to the sovereignty and majesty and glory of God. They worshipped.

What Paul and Silas experienced was extreme, but not necessarily uncommon. It reminds me of what I see happening in Haiti. People devastated by an earthquake, people who have endured unspeakable loss and suffering, and yet, they worship. Multiple scenes on the news reveal people with lifted hands, praising God and singing. How? They did what they knew would encourage them.

Life sometimes bombards us with circumstances beyond belief, circumstances that appear to be outside the realm of God's goodness. Perhaps not an earthquake, but in those moments, we have a choice. We can blame God, which in some respects, is the natural choice. If God is in charge, then one could reason He must be responsible. We can accuse him, in anger, "God, this is your fault. You did this. How could you?"

However, blaming God doesn't get you anywhere. If you choose to blame God, your hope is stripped away and you are left without answers. Blaming God when you don't understand why something difficult had to happen is essentially bringing God down to your level. Now God is no wiser or more powerful that you are. You are not allowing God to be sovereign—to be in control. In effect, you are saying, "God, I can't come up with a good reason for this, therefore, there must not be one. You couldn't possibly know more or see more than I do." Not a good place to be—kind of scary in fact. Rather than admitting that God has a plan that we cannot see, it's easier to lash out.

I am not suggesting we don't express our feelings to God. If Jesus cried out from the cross and asked a very hard question ("My God, my God, why have you forsaken me?"), then so can we. However, we don't want to go so far as to allow our doubting to eliminate the hope of His gracious sovereignty. God is in control of all things, but we live in a world where the prince of darkness still reigns. Many times, that's the reason we experience hardship. We live in the midst of human darkness and sin. It's tough, but don't let that turn your view of God into one that is cruel and heartless, when, in fact, God has sacrificed Himself to defeat those very things.

Remember, there is another option besides blame. When life is hard, we have another choice—faith. We can choose to remember who God is and all that He's promised us. Just as

Paul and Silas demonstrated—rather than blame—we can worship. In moments of fear and doubt, we need encouragement. We need to be reminded of what is true. When you make the choice to worship, you are acknowledging and accepting God's eternal promises to see you through the valley.

In Psalm 43:4, while facing the perils of leadership, David writes, "....for I will yet praise him, my Savior and my God." Even in the midst of struggle, "I will yet praise Him." David made the same choice as Paul and Silas, to worship, even though he didn't understand God's master plan at the time. When we take time to bow before the Lord, to offer Him praise and adoration, to confess our sins, and sing of His wonders, it allows us to remember that God has not caused the evil, but instead has answered it in Jesus Christ. Worship creates space for us to reflect on the fact that sin and death still reign, but Christ is yet to return! God still patiently waits so that more might receive him. Worship tells us that Christ is the victor. Christ is risen! And so we sing. We pray. We dive into the Word, for by doing so, we offer an internal witness to our soul of the unyielding power and presence of God. We don't think of this as much as we should, but when we worship, we witness to ourselves. It is an internal witness to our soul.

Horatio Spafford was a successful Chicago attorney and businessman in the mid-1800s. He was active in the Presbyterian Church as a lay servant and also helped lead the Chicago YMCA in its earliest years. As his life progressed, he endured a number of hardships, including the Great Chicago Fire. By 1873, his wife's health had started to fail and a doctor suggested a vacation. Spafford decided on a trip to England so that his family could hear the great Dwight L. Moody preach. In the fall of that year, Spafford put his wife, Anna, and his four daughters, Maggie, Tanetta, Annie and Bessie, on a ship bound for England. He planned to wrap up some business and join them a few days later. But it was not to be. On November 22, 1873, the S.S. Ville du Havre was struck off the coast of Newfoundland by an English ship. It sank in twelve minutes, taking 226 lives, including all four of Spafford's daughters. His wife, Anna, cabled him a two word message: "Saved alone."

Days later, as Spafford sailed the very same route to meet his grief-stricken wife, he was notified by the captain that they were near the site of the crash. In that moment, he went out to the rails and penned the words to the hymn, "*It is Well With My Soul.*" Having just lost his four daughters, Spafford wrote, (When peace like a river, attendeth my way, when sorrows like sea billows roll; whatever my lot, Thou hast taught me to say, 'It is well, it is well, with my soul.')

In that moment, despite tragedy and death, Spafford expressed a heart of worship. He was laid bare before the Lord. He expressed his pain and sorrow, yet in worship, he allowed the Spirit of God to speak into his heart. As he reflected on the nature of God, he was assured again that whether in peace or adversity, his soul was well. God was faithful. God was still on the throne. This is the power of worship. It does not mean we ignore our feelings or pretend that everything is fine when it's not. Rather, we take the time to recapture what is true, even when little else makes sense. It means we return to the core of our relationship with God: worship. Worship is never a rote, perfunctory duty. It is a spiritual discipline which we cannot live without.

Worship as Outward Witness

Not only does worship serve as an inward witness, but it also bears an outward witness. When Paul and Silas were worshiping God, they were not the only ones involved. The text reminds us of what the prisoners were doing. As amazing as it sounds, they listened.

In order to grasp the magnitude of those two words, you have to understand the nature of the environment. This was a jail in every sense of the word. When Paul and Silas were dragged into the jail, the other prisoners were not rolling out the welcome mat. It was harsh and ugly and cruel. Language was perverse and vulgar. Self-preservation was the rule. Violence was common. Yet, even in that context, the language of worship rose, and those nearby took note. They listened. They did not object. They did not condemn. They did not shout contradictions. They listened. I believe they did so because what they heard bore witness of God's love and His truth. It was radically different from anything they had ever heard in jail before, and as a result, it captured them.

What's more, their worship led to the miraculous opening of the jail doors and the conversion of the jailer. In Acts 16:30, the jailer asks, "What must I do to be saved?" In other words,

"I want to have what you have." Their worship bore witness to the power of God such that others around them wanted to share in it. Remember, Lydia was saved by going to worship. The prisoners were attentive to the sounds of worship. The jailer is saved by the power of worship. In just this one chapter, over and over again, God is illustrating the transforming power of worship. It is time for us and for our churches to reclaim that power! Our worship bears witness to those who are hungry to find life. Worship can create a hunger for Christ. It is never an inward witness alone. It is not just for us. It also bears an outward witness to others.

To be clear, just because worship bears an outward witness does not mean everyone will respond positively. It is quite likely people will think us odd and misguided. So be it. We are called to continue as God has commanded us. However, if we understand our worship as an outward witness, we must also realize that it can be a negative witness if we are not unified. Through worship, we have the power to build the Kingdom of God, but we also have the power to harm it.

As I discussed in the last chapter, rather than bearing witness through worship, many Christian communities are being divided by worship. Much time and attention are focused on making worship feel comfortable for the unchurched. We spend huge amounts of energy trying to understand what will "attract" a particular person or demographic to worship. As a result, we offer a variety of forms of worship to attract our target audiences. For teenagers, we put colorful images on computer screens and flash laser lights. We throw information at them in rapid succession because, we are told, this is how to best reach them. For young adults, we select music and prayers and liturgy that are participatory and authentic so they can more readily engage in an experience. For this group, we do this, for that group, we do that—and on and on it goes.

While I believe there is value in the discussion, let me be clear: we do not need to radically alter the Gospel in order to accommodate the feelings of any generation. The *form* of worship is not what transforms people; lives are transformed when God so moves the hearts of the people gathered that they worship passionately, openly, and authentically. A particular format or style of worship can help us do that, but form is not the only ingredient. It is much more a matter of heart.

When we worship with all of our hearts, we become alive. As a result, the churches in which we worship will become places that bear outward witness to all who enter. Let me give you an example. We had a service some time ago in which God did some amazing things. Three teens in the service were profoundly changed, and they left that day full of the hope of Christ. They told their friends about what they had experienced in worship. Several weeks later, they brought one of their friends, who received Christ that day. In my conversation with that young woman, she talked openly about the change she had witnessed in her friends, the enthusiasm and love which they shared, and her deep desire to find the same thing.

I realize, it doesn't always happen that way, but it can. In a perfect world, Christians could be confident bringing a non-believer to a worship service, knowing that they would be moved by the Spirit of God because it was so evident—so alive—and so real in that place. In a perfect world, non-believers would respond to worship by asking, "How can I have what this body has?"

A Challenge to Our Worship

As I study the powerful events of Acts 16, I am forced to consider my own worship and the worship of the community in which I serve. What kind of witness does my worship bear to me and to the world? What kind of witness does my church bear when we worship?

As a pastor, there are times when I wish my congregation could see themselves during worship. I would love to project their faces up on the screen just so they could have a look. It would be much like what happens during timeouts at an Orlando Magic game. There is a "kiss cam" that searches the crowd looking for couples, and if you wind up on the scoreboard, you have to kiss the person you are with. (It leads to some very funny exchanges between couples!) In the same way, I would love to have a "worship cam." How enlightening it would be for us to see one another as we engage in worship. Some yawn. Some look as though their dog has just been run over by a car. Some fidget and look at their watches. Some have that far away look that says they are already planning the agenda for their Monday morning meeting. There are some, however, who truly look like they are standing in the presence of God. They are the ones I find myself being drawn back to when I lead from the front. Their faces encourage and inspire me, and I find myself worshiping in a more meaningful way. That's what I want. That's what I pray for.

Real worship should be about linking our hearts to the everlasting God. As such, we should sing and pray and respond because we are engaged with God. When we take part in or hear a Scripture reading, it should not be some kind of empty lament, but rather the truth of our hearts. When we sing a hymn or praise song, we should sing because the words resonate with the desire and longing of our hearts. To be sure, if there is no truth or hope in us, then we will not sing. We will not worship because we have nothing to sing about. However, when we realize that God in Christ is alive and at work; when we realize He has reached into the darkness of our lives and brought hope, *then* we can truly begin to worship. When that happens, we will begin to bear witness to Christ's love to all who enter, and those lives—and ours—will be changed.

I will never forget the first year I spent as a senior pastor. I was at Covenant Presbyterian Church in Ft. Myers, Florida, a church that had been wounded and divided over a number of issues just prior to my arrival. The first few months were long. Trust levels were low. In the midst of the challenges and pain and difficulty, I preached on the power of the Holy Spirit on Pentecost Sunday. At the end of the service, I did something that is a bit unusual in most mainline churches. I gave an invitation. I asked that anyone who had not professed faith in Christ as their Savior and Lord and who desired to be baptized to come forward as the last hymn was sung. I'll never forget the looks on their faces. No one would make eye contact with me. Heads were dropped. People were fidgeting. I was standing at the head of the center aisle, in front of the communion table—alone.

As the new guy, it felt like everyone was thinking, "What is this guy trying to do?" I honestly don't remember what hymn we sang. I just remember that for the first three verses, everyone stood squarely in their spot, unmoving. The longer it went, the more antsy and uncomfortable people became. Then, as we started verse four, from the back row, a single young woman stepped out and began to walk that long aisle forward. She met me at the steps and with tears in her eyes, told me that she had not been in a church in many years, but for some reason, felt compelled to come on that day. Her name was Kerry, and she said her experience in worship had changed her: "I feel God's love and presence. I want to receive Christ and be baptized."

In all my years, I don't know that I have felt joy the way I did in that moment. I stopped the singing and asked the congregation to be seated. I then asked her a series of questions that allowed her to state her faith before the body. Having shared her heart, our elders came forward and gathered around her, and I baptized her. You should have seen the looks on the faces of all those people. Mouths were literally hanging open. They could not believe what they had just witnessed. When I completed the baptism, the elders returned to their seats, but then a strange thing happened. No one was in a rush to get home. All 500 of us stayed well past the hour (which for Presbyterians is a big deal) and we worshiped. A palpable sense of joy took over the room. We sang and we prayed. As people sang, they would turn and smile at each other. They had just witnessed God change someone's heart. It was as sweet and tender a time of worship as I have ever had, and to this day, there is not a Pentecost Sunday that goes by when I do not think of Kerry's courage and the profound impact she had on our church. She was transformed by the Holy Spirit in worship and as a result of her transformation, an entire body was impacted.

My prayer for you and for the Church of Jesus Christ is that we will begin to cultivate that kind of heart in worship. A heart that realizes worship is not a Sunday-only thing, but an all-the-time state of mind. Through worship, we bear witness to our souls and to the souls of those around us. It is a witness to the power and grace of God which changes lives. I don't have all the answers to the issues facing the church today, but I do know this: if we want to be healthy and authentic in our Christian walk—if we want to experience the life that Jesus promised—then worship must be at the center of our experience. It must be something we understand and practice, both individually and corporately. As we do, God is honored and His body grows. I yearn for moments like I had that morning at 3 a.m. May He bless us all with more glimpses of His glory!

6

"Our major task in life is to discover what is true and to live in step with that truth."

CHUCK COLSON, *HOW NOW SHALL WE LIVE*

"False ideas are the greatest obstacles to the reception of the gospel. We may preach with all the fervor of a reformer and yet succeed only in winning a straggler here or there, if we permit the whole collective thought of a nation or of the world to be controlled by ideas which by the resistless force of logic, prevent Christianity from being regarded as anything more than a harmless delusion."

J. GRESHAM MACHEN

"Let the word of Christ dwell in you richly"

COLOSSIANS 3:16

Not long ago, I watched an amazing YouTube video. A group of college students had taken numerous bottles of soda and lined them up along the ground in multiple rows. With symphonic music playing in the background, they rhythmically dropped Mentos breath mints in the bottles, in time with the music, sending the soda soaring from each one like a geyser. It was creative, messy and fun, but I wasn't sure whether or not it was real.

It could have easily been a hoax; I figured the only way to really know for sure was to test it myself. Thus, armed with a soda and a roll of Mentos, I headed out to my backyard. I must have had a "mad scientist" look about me, because my wife was completely puzzled.

My little experiment proved very educational. Upon dropping several Mentos into a bottle of Diet Coke, there was an enormous spray of soda cascading over my head. It worked! I had tested the authenticity of what I had seen, proven it to be true and in so doing, become a believer. In many respects, this echoes our daily struggle.

Whether consciously or unconsciously, we are all trying to uncover what is true. We live and make choices based on what we think is true. We all have a belief system, whether we can articulate it or not, and that belief system guides our actions as we try to live in step with our truth. In considering the question of why so many Christians profess faith but do not live in abundance, I think the notion of truth is critical to the discussion. We say we believe that Christianity is true, but do our choices and behaviors reflect that belief? Are we living according to God's truth, or do we only give it lip service while living according to our own truth? If we are going to live vital, healthy, Christian lives, rich with the abundance promised in Jesus Christ, one of the most important things we can do is align our lives with what is *true.*

An Elusive Goal

Often, truth can be hard to find, but every once in awhile you discover it bubbling up in the strangest of places. It may be thinly veiled, but all the sudden, there it is! Believe it or not, for several years now, I've found the gospel in a series of commercials on network television. Particularly, a recent Gatorade ad campaign. Each spot featured an athlete reaching extreme exhaustion while participating in their sport of choice. A boxer, locked in what appears to be mortal combat, mercilessly punching his opponent, while sweat flies in every which direction; a gymnast straining to support herself on the balance beam, grimacing as sweat beads up on her forehead; football players slamming into each other with bone-jarring force, sweat-soaked helmets flying. In one particularly grotesque scene, a runner doubles over a park bench, hair plastered to her head, dripping with sweat, and throws up. As the athletes pause to rehydrate, in addition to the sweat pouring from their faces and bodies, something else appears: a different, brightly-colored liquid, (the same color as the sport drink they are consuming) trickling down their faces. Finally, with pictures of these highly conditioned athletes still pumping away, the commercial asks, "Is it in you?" Obviously, the ad is suggesting that Gatorade makes it possible for the athletes to accomplish such feats of endurance and skill, and perhaps could have the same effect for anyone watching at home. All I can say is that, so far, it hasn't worked for me.

I think the campaign asks a wonderful, almost disturbing, question: what, exactly, is in us? The commercial suggests a profound truth. What you put in your body will, more than likely, come out in some way. What you put in your body impacts what your body is able to do. It's true, from a physical perspective. But it's also true in other dimensions. What we put into our bodies, what we allow into our minds, how we fill our spirits, it is all bound to have an impact on what our lives produce.

The old axiom is true: garbage in, garbage out. Truth in, truth out. In Galatians 6, Paul said, "A man reaps what he sows." Science has given us ample evidence to support this truth. We know with great certainty that if we smoke, we will increase our odds for developing cancer and long-term respiratory problems. When smoke and nicotine go in, what comes out is generally not too good. If we put fatty foods loaded with cholesterol in our mouths, we will end up with clogged arteries.

We are only now beginning to understand the influence of television, computers and video games on our children. Recent studies have shown a link between the increase in juvenile violence and the repetitive nature of killing in video games. (Craig Anderson, Karen Dill, *Journal of Personality and Social Psychology*, 2000.) We will reap what we sow. If this is true, if there is some correlation between what we put into our lives and what comes out of them, then we must identify what we are putting into our lives and our hearts. We must make sure the truth is in us.

Filled Up

This is exactly what Paul is talking about in Colossians 3:16, a verse which I quoted at the start of the chapter. Paul is cautioning the Colossian Christians about what they were putting in their lives, and offering words of correction about how they needed to change. As you think about this, try to grasp the communications of Paul's day as compared to now. We text, email, and instant message one another all the time. My children can move their thumbs over their cell phone keypads at speeds beyond my imagination. We get responses to online inquiries in seconds.

Naturally, the speed of our communication affects the nature of our responses. If someone asked you a question today and you knew you would not be able to hear back from that person for months—if you knew this was your one chance to tell them what you thought—you would be more intentional and cautious about your choice of words. You would answer more thoughtfully, and in some cases, more strategically. That was Paul's world. Communication was slow. It took weeks and sometimes months to send or receive messages. Given Paul's wisdom and leadership, he was often consulted by churches for help in crisis situations and most of his letters in the New Testament are believed to be answers to communications he had received. Such was the case with this letter to the Colossians. Something was happening that was causing significant problems, and Paul was consulted for guidance. He wanted to answer them, and because of the infrequency of communication, he chose his words very carefully. He crafted a powerful argument for the Colossian church to wrestle with, and it remains a powerful argument for the church today. It's an argument for truth.

At the time, the Colossian church was literally being overrun with false teachers. Without getting sidetracked in the details, these teachers were promoting an amalgamation of cultural thought, pagan deities, and early Christian theology. They believed in spirits called "eons" that controlled all of human life. These spirits were found in everything on earth and in the heavens—trees, plants, stars, rocks, wind, bugs—all of it. In a word, it was polytheism. In regard to Jesus, they believed he was just one of many spirits to be worshiped and praised in order to attain salvation and the promise of a good life. Jesus was by no means unique, simply one spirit among many.

You can imagine how confusing it was for the church to hear this. Paul says, in Colossians 2:18, that these teachers were led by a human way of thinking, that they had "a mind of the flesh." In a commentary on Colossians, Ralph Martin wrote, "The nature of this teaching was a composite and was made up partly of Jewish elements and partly ideas belonging to the world of Hellenistic religious philosophy and mysticism." Sound familiar? It should. It's the same situation we find ourselves in today.

The collective wisdom of our culture is setting the standard for truth, and the church is buying into it. Thus, as the culture changes, so does our understanding of truth. It's a constantly moving target. This temptation to abide by secular truths haunted the Colossian church and it remains an issue for the church today. The culture was influencing the doctrine of the church instead of the other way around. As a result, the Colossian church was being tempted away from Christ as Savior and towards a variety of gods. Works, not grace, were required, and only a select few seemed to know which works did the trick. In effect, these teachers put the human mind in a position of authority rather than the mind of Christ. They were putting false things in and as a result, what was coming out was not a life, or a church, which honored God.

An Honest Rebuke

Thankfully, Paul didn't mince words. He was straight up with the Colossians about the reality of how they were living and what their lives were producing: "Put to death therefore, whatever belongs to your earthly nature: sexual immorality, lust, greed, impurity, anger, malice, slander, and filthy language. You used to walk in these ways." (Colossians 3:5-7) If he is telling them to put these things to death, the implication is they were still very much alive.

The Colossian Christians were alive, but they were living according to their earthly natures. Because of their worldly understanding of truth, they were living lives of disobedience and darkness. Please don't ignore this point. Don't let yourself off the hook too easily. It is more comfortable to sit back right now and say, "Well, that's not me" or "I know I'm putting all the right things in my life." Really? Think about it. Think about how you define truth and whether you live by that truth. What in your life may need to change?

The principle is clear: if you put things in your life that are false—things that are not of Christ—your life will reflect behavior that is not of Christ. Your life will actually produce fruit that is harmful to you and to the body of Christ. If you're like me, sometimes you step back and look at your own life and wonder, "How did I get here? How did this happen?" It is in those moments that I often realize I wasn't following truth. I was following my own truth.

We need get to rid of that kind of thinking. We need to stop putting what is false in our hearts, but the standards of our world have become so alarmingly lax and we fall right in line. What we see in movies and television today would not have been tolerated 25 years ago, but we don't think anything of it now. Our world pats itself on the back and pronounces itself "progressive." We get sucked right in. I know it sounds like a parent talking to a child, but sometimes, I think I need to hear it loud and clear, "Stop it! Stop doing that! Stop filling your heart with worldly trash!"

The image Paul uses is that of clothing. Because of what the Colossians had put in their hearts, they were producing external lives that needed to be stripped away. It's as if they were literally cloaked in sin. Instead, as people loved by God, Paul says, "Put on compassion, kindness, humility, gentleness and patience. Forgive and love—be at peace and be thankful." I don't think we would disagree with that. I think, in our hearts, that's the life we want. We want a life where we feel compassion for others. We want a life where we are truly humble. We know those qualities are good, strong qualities. We know the aforementioned qualities are dangerous and destructive. Yet, it still begs the question, "How can we produce a good life?" I know I would choose the life of kindness and gentleness if I could, but I know that's not the life I have now. So, if I don't have it, how can I get it? How can I produce that life?

A New Input

Paul does not leave us empty handed. He answers that question in a powerful way. He says, "Let the word of Christ dwell in you richly as you teach and admonish one another...." Once again, we are back to what we are putting into our lives. To borrow from a business model known as "systems theory," if you run a company that produces widgets, and there is a flaw in the widgets produced, you have to check your system. You can't expect good outputs if your inputs are substandard. It will simply never work. That's what Paul is telling us. Check your system and change your inputs! If you want to live the life that you desire and actually experience the abundance Christ promises, then you need to change your inputs. You need to stop putting the things of the world inside your heart and start filling it with the things of God—start filling it with His word!

Paul is sharing the most fundamental, central truth of Christian faith and doctrine. If we are going to produce Christ-like lives as God so desires (Ephesians 1); if we are going to produce what is good and right and pure; if we are going to produce lives which are satisfying and rich, we must first put something in us that will produce that result. We must allow the word of God to dwell in us richly and deeply. If we have any notion that the Christian Church can change the world, if we have any hope that we can make a difference in the pain we see around us, then we have to change what we are putting into it—*and that starts with what we as individuals consume.* For Paul, this is the very center of the Christian life and ministry. We must consume the Word of God and make it part of us.

A Tall Order
That directive, of course, leads to an honest question: how? What does it mean to put the word of God in us? Paul helps us with that question, too. First, we have to allow God's word to "dwell" in us. The Greek word for "dwell" is the word "oikos" which likens our lives to a home. The word of God is to come and be "at home" in our lives. It is to "inhabit" our lives completely.

When I think about my own life, I am not sure I can say that is entirely true. I don't know that the word of God is "at home" or "makes its dwelling" in me. What a challenge! Several summers ago when I attended the Christian Life Conference, my family rented a house in Montreat, North Carolina with two other families. It was a much-needed vacation and an opportunity to be with others we loved. Needless to say, we were very excited about going. Even so, it was a challenging dynamic as among our three families we had eight children under the age of nine. At best, it was going to be chaotic.

As the "planner" of the group, it was my responsibility to find an appropriate home to rent for the week. Obviously, we needed a lot of space and a lot of bathrooms. I did my due diligence, made some calls, talked to some realtors, went online, and finally decided on a nice five-bedroom house. It looked great in the photographs and appeared to have everything we needed, so I signed the papers. However, I made one catastrophic error: I never actually went inside the house. When we arrived that first day, we discovered the house was sorely lacking. It had only one shower, no air conditioning, no linens or towels, and no utensils. It did, however, have one thing in spades: Mold. Yes, mold. To say that I lost some popularity with my friends would be an understatement. My wife, in her most pastoral tone, kept asking me, "Did you not read the specifications about this house? Did you not read the rental agreement?" Trying to make the best of a bad situation, we thought we would just give it a good cleaning. However, even with our best elbow grease, we realized we were no match for the mold. It was in the vents, up the walls, in the furniture. It was pervasive. Even in the smallest, tiniest crevices, it would show up. We coughed and hacked for two days and then finally, we gave up and went home. The mold inhabiting the house had started to inhabit us as well.

This is exactly what Paul is talking about. When something "dwells" in our lives it should be everywhere. It should be pervasive—every area, every room, every thought, every notion. Let it dwell there. Let it live there, because, when it does, it will begin to change what seeps out of your life. It will change you from the inside out. When the word of God inhabits your life, you will find it is the One who keeps setting the trash by the door; the One who opens the windows to allow for fresh air to come in; the One who keeps leaving notes on the bathroom mirrors reminding you to trust and love and obey.

I do pretty well at allowing the word to dwell in my living room, my den, my kitchen—but I don't do as well at allowing it to dwell in the smallest, darkest corners of my life. There are just some places where I don't want to give up control. We all have places that we don't want to yield. We all have places that we like to keep dirty. It's our sinful nature hard at work. Yet, if we let our sinful nature go unchecked, we have to understand it *will* affect our ability to live abundantly. There cannot be one area—not even one crack—where we do not allow the word of God to dwell. To borrow the image from the classic *My Heart, Christ's Home*, we need to let God's word dwell in the entirety of our lives—the *whole* house.

While it appears a daunting challenge, and perhaps one we will never attain this side of heaven, it is one that we can grow in, a goal we can move towards. The key is found in one little word in the text—one little, but very important, word. A seminary professor once asked his class, "What is the most important word in all of Scripture?" Students responded with words like love, salvation, prayer and grace, but finally he said, "No. It is a little three letter word - *let*." Throughout the Bible, the word "let" is an invitation to throw open some door inside ourselves to what God wants to do in us, but we have to allow it. We have to open it. We have to *let* God in. Here, God says, "*let* the word of Christ dwell in you richly."

Anne Graham Lotz was interviewed by Larry King shortly after the 9/11 attacks. He asked her where God was in the midst of the terrorist attacks. At one point, she said, "God is a gentleman." I love that side of God's character. He is a gentleman. If we reject God over and over again, He won't force Himself on us. He won't force obedience or love. We have the freedom to reject Him if we so choose. We're not robots. We are free, choosing agents. If we weren't, God would not hold us accountable for our actions. No doubt these choices fall under His sovereignty and God enacts His purpose regardless of what we decide. However, we still have to choose to let God dwell in us. We have to let Him abide in us. We have to let His Word in. We have to decide what to put in our lives—and God very gently says, "Let it be my word."

The Foundation for Life

Paul doesn't stop there. He goes on. He says we are to allow the Word to inhabit our lives. Then, he moves on to the larger body of the church. He says let the word dwell in you "as you teach and admonish one another with all wisdom and as you sing spiritual songs to God...." Remember, Paul was writing to correct the false teaching that had infected the Colossian church, so not only were they encouraged to "put the word" in their personal lives, but more than that, make it the foundation of their teaching and their worship.

I love this about our calling as Christians. We are never called into isolation. God does not give you the blessing of your salvation so you can run off and sit in a corner and be satisfied with it. He calls you to be a part of a larger whole— the body of Christ. You are blessed, yes, but you are still one part of a larger whole—and your part in that whole is significant! As the word dwells in you, you are called to make it the building block—the foundation—of Christ's Church. Let the word of God dwell in you as you teach. Let the word of God dwell in you as you sing songs—as you worship. Let the word of God dwell in you as you admonish and encourage one another in relationships. As you are together—as you are the church—let the word dwell in you.

In an article in *Christianity Today*, Jean Fleming wrote, "In the Scriptures, God reveals Himself to us, shapes the life of Christ in us, and extends the work of Christ through us." As we forge and shape the future of the body, His Church, we do so in the hope that God will reveal Himself to us—shape the life of Christ in us—and extend the work of Christ through us as we serve each other, our communities, and our world." Therefore, as we think about what we do—how we shape our lives and ministry—we must strive to be centered on God's Word. Sure, there are wonderful things that we could be taught. We could sign up for classes to learn about woodworking, foreign languages, or classic literature. That's all great, but what are we doing so that we internalize the word of God? Our churches can teach classes on philosophy, global warming, or the worldview of William Shakespeare, but that is not the church's unique call. The unique call of God is for the church to teach Scripture. We do that because the Scriptures are the only living word—the only word capable of working in us to effect change to the glory of God.

Once again, this gets to the core of our original question: why is it that so many who profess faith in Jesus Christ never live in the spiritual abundance He promised? Part of the answer is found here—in whether or not our foundation is rooted in the word of God. If we want to be empowered for mission and service—if we want to be able to "put on" qualities like love and compassion and kindness—then God's truth must inhabit us. It must inhabit our churches. If we want to produce a life abundant with the things of God, we must put His truth in us.

In the same way, if we want churches that are alive with the Spirit of God, we must be putting truth in them. Many people have asked me why our culture keeps getting further from the truth, and even beyond that, why so many churches seem to be adopting cultural norms. Why are some churches blessing same-sex unions? Why are some churches advocating a theology of Jesus that says Jesus is but one way among many to salvation? The answer is exactly what we're talking about.

We have allowed the shifting truth of our culture to trump the truth of God's word. We have slipped into a theological understanding of Scripture as merely a book of wisdom, rather than one which holds eternal and absolute authority.

These days, it is a widely held belief that the individual stands above Scripture, determining what is relevant and what is not. Like Thomas Jefferson and his "Jefferson Bible," we pick the parts we like and cut out the parts we don't. To the contrary, we are to sit beneath the authority of God's word—infallible in every respect—and plant it deeply in our hearts. This is the church's unique call. Thus, as I think about the church I lead, this truth governs my choices. It is why in Sunday school, for both adults and children, we endeavor to teach Scripture. It is why we want to build a network of small groups, so that through Bible study, we can nurture a love for and knowledge of God's word in the hearts of our congregants. It is why we teach Scripture to our children and ask our confirmation classes to memorize passages. It is why we build our youth and college ministries around Scripture. We want the word of God to come alive! We're teaching the Bible because it is only when we make God's word the foundation of our lives that we will be able to fulfill our calling to serve Him and truly live faithful, abundant lives.

Paul also tells us that worship should be centered on His word. When we gather together on Sunday to sing songs and praise God, we are allowing His word to dwell in us. It is why we place the Bible in the center of our communion table, as a reminder of its central place in our lives. It is why my sermons are based on the teachings of Scripture. A sermon should never be just my thoughts or ideas; it must be more than something that tickles the ears, more than cute stories and sweet sentiments. The word of God is what separates bone and marrow or as it says in Hebrews 4, joint and muscle. It is sharp and penetrating, hopeful and comforting, joyous and scary—the word of God is all these things. As such, we must allow it to permeate our worship. For only then are we being obedient—only then are we being changed.

This is one of the greatest problems in the church today: an acute lack of biblical preaching. Often, preachers will start a message by reading the Scripture, but that is the last you ever hear of it. Without returning to God's word, the sermon becomes the preacher's collection of wisdom and thoughts.

Regardless of how smart or charismatic, a preacher's understanding of truth is not going to change the world. It has no
authority. I want to know what God has said is true. I want
the preacher to expound the word of God, because that word
does have authority and *can* change me.

In today's current culture, with its variety of worship
styles and architectures, many churches have lost one of the
great symbols of their heritage: the pulpit. In the old churches
of Scotland, the pulpit was located in the center of the sanctuary—high and ornate—above the communion table. It was
not a symbol of the status of the preacher, but rather a reminder of the place where God's word came forth. God's word was
to be high and lifted up, viewed and heard with great respect.
We were to raise our eyes to it, hallow it, and revere it. Somewhere along the way, that concept was forgotten and we began lifting up the preachers themselves. I'm not saying we all
need to bring back pulpits, but I do think we need to reclaim
the significance of God's word in our worship.

Truth, in Abundance

We have learned much from Paul's words to the Colossian
Christians as well as his encouragement of that church's life
and ministry. His advice is quite simple. God's word must
dwell in us and in our churches. It must be the focus of our
teaching, our worship and our relationships with one another.
If we are faithful in this, then what flows out of our churches
will be the living waters of Christ. Living water will flow from
us because living water is *in* us.

Still, a question remains: is it enough? Is Scripture really
enough to change and sustain me? Given the nature of my
current circumstances, is it enough? It is a fair question. In
my experience, sometimes the answer can only be learned
through the real challenges of life. Paul would say, "Yes, it
is enough." He said we are to allow God's word to dwell in
us "richly." What Paul is trying to communicate is the abundant, sufficient nature of God's word. The Greek word in
this text, translated as "richly," literally means, "abundantly
available or overflowing." In other words, there will always
be enough for us, regardless of our need, if we allow God's
word to dwell in us.

To be clear, that does not mean we will not suffer pain or
that all our prayers will be answered immediately. However,

it does allow us to draw close to the presence of God, to experience His power to sustain us through all things—and to
minister to others. In his book, *The Things That Matter Most*,
John Henry Jowett wrote, "When the Divine life possesses the
soul, it flows over in gracious ministries among our fellow
man. The affluence becomes an influence importing itself into
the lives of others." When the Word of God dwells in us, it
is indeed rich. It is so abundant in us that it overflows from
our lives into our world. Our affluence becomes influence in
others and in our communities. It is enough provision to meet
our every need if we will allow it to dwell in our lives.

Everybody's Looking

No question, people are desperate to find truth. Whether it's
Oprah, the latest self-help bestseller or a new political phe-
nom, people want something that will solve their problems
and make their lives easier. Our world is searching, almost
desperately, to find something that is true—something they
can depend on—and the search has become so desperate that
they are willing to try anything, regardless of how misguided
it may be. I believe the time is ripe for the truth of God to be
shared. People are searching for what is true, and thankfully,
we have it.

According to a 2006 *New York Times* article, more people
die each year from unsafe drinking water than from all other
forms of violence, including war. More than a billion people—one in every five on earth—must search for places that
have safe drinking water because it is not readily available.
This creates a dangerous situation. They are thirsty, but the
available water is not safe. It might kill them, so what do they
do? People die because they are thirsty and the only water
they can find—despite looking clean and perhaps even tasting fine—will kill them. Like the athletes in the commercial
I described earlier, we come to the wells of this world exhausted from the battles and circumstances we face. We're
thirsty. We're looking for something that can quench our
thirst, something that will sustain us and strengthen us. In
the process, we are tempted to satisfy our thirst by drinking
from things that look good, and may even taste good, but in
the end only lead to our destruction. The Colossian church
wrestled with the false teaching of their day, and today, we

face the same temptations as we try to live in the midst of a spiritually changing culture.

I want to live a vital life. I want a life that is producing good things, the things of God's own heart. To do that, I know I have to put the right things in me. It requires my action and my effort. I must challenge myself to do that everyday and I want to challenge you as well. Are you in a Bible study? If you're not, get in one. If you don't go to a Sunday School class or some other educational ministry like Bible Study Fellowship or Community Bible Study, start going. If you don't have a daily devotional life, ask someone for help. Consult with your pastor or a friend about their disciplines. Find out what devotional books or tools help them to spend time with God and in His word each day. Then, get started. Make it a habit. Examine your life closely and do what is necessary to find the right inputs. Think about what your life is producing. Think about what you want your life to produce. Then ask yourself, "is it in you?"

7

SM ✓

EXERCISING FAITH:
A COMMITMENT TO MINISTRY AND MISSION

*"We loved you so much that we were delighted to
share with you not only the gospel of God but our
lives as well."*

1 THESSALONIANS 2:8

*"...(there are) those today who worry only about
whether they can afford the new SUV and still pay
for the new bathroom, soccer camp, and having
their teeth whitened. Then they worry that they
will need a better job to afford all these things.....
and that gets them worrying about how to make
the next move.....There is simply no room in their
hearts left...."*

CRAIG BARNES, *SEARCHING FOR HOME*

"Who despises the day of small things?"

ZECHARIAH 4:10

SM

I first met Scott in the summer of 1990 while working as a
chaplain at Seton Medical Center in Austin, Texas. He was 25,
tall and lanky with a full head of blond hair and an outgoing
charisma that made him very easy to be around. Fresh out of
graduate school at the University of Texas, and looking for a
job as an engineer, Scott was as nice a person as you'd ever
meet. He was also gay and infected with the HIV virus that
had advanced into full-blown AIDS.

I first encountered him at the hospital as he came in to
get blood work for a cough he couldn't shake, and after that,
I kept an eye out for him. He would come in every two or
three weeks, sometimes looking better, sometimes looking
worse, but always positive, always upbeat, and always genuinely glad to see me. We struck up what I thought was a good
friendship. I tried to listen as best I could. I asked questions
about his faith. We talked openly and honestly about a lot of
things. However, as time went on, I began to realize a rather

sad truth. He was alone. In spite of his charismatic charm, no one ever came with him. I never saw him interacting in another human relationship. It was completely odd to me. He did talk about a dog and a cat, but that was all he ever shared.

As time went on, his illness progressed until, sadly, he was checked into the hospital. He had gotten pneumonia along with a horrific skin cancer common to AIDS patients called Kaposi's Sarcoma. As a result, huge purple sores broke out all over his body. It was ugly and debilitating and tremendously uncomfortable. Up to that point, I had never seen a man suffer that much.

In the quiet of that hospital room, even in his pain, we continued to talk and share. We talked more about his family—about his relationships—and in the process, I discovered why I never saw any other people with him. Every single person in his life—everyone who had ever meant anything to him—had, in effect, disowned him. His parents had walked away when he announced he was gay. Scott's partner fled when he was diagnosed HIV positive. His other friends did not want to be around him because his illness scared them; it was too real, too close to home. He had no one.

Knowing this, I did all I could to spend more time with him, trying to provide emotional and spiritual support. I must confess, the more time I spent with him, the more I fully expected someone to come walking through the door—a relative, an old friend—someone. But no one ever did. Six weeks later, Scott died in that hospital room, and he died alone. No family ever came. No friends. No loved ones. Here was a man whose life had come to an end—a painful, agonizing end—and it was as if no one cared. A life had passed from this earth, and it didn't even seem to register. Scott's life had not mattered enough for anyone to come—or even notice.

I wonder at times if we live our lives in the same way. We live in a self-absorbed culture where we work hard to meet our own needs, accomplish our own goals and solve our own problems. As such, we simply don't have time for others. We cross paths with people on a daily basis who are dying—destined for darkness—and it really doesn't effect us, primarily because we don't notice. We're quite happy with our own lives—our homes, our jobs, our relationships. We're quite content to head down to our church on Sunday mornings and see some people we know and hear about God's love for us.

We head out for brunch and enjoy a nice meal. We discuss the sermon as it pertains to our lives and we quietly put it away, satisfied that we are walking and abiding in God's will.

Meanwhile, the person reeling from divorce who barely mustered the courage to come to church, a person yearning for a kind word from someone, passed you in the hall and got nothing. The waitress who served you lunch just put her mother in a home for Alzheimer's patients, but you wouldn't know that because you didn't take the time to ask. Your neighbor, out working in the yard, just heard that his brother has terminal cancer. He has no faith whatsoever and his mind is filled with confusing questions about death and dying, but you wouldn't know that because, well, the game was coming on in ten minutes and you really needed to get inside.

Is this where we are as individuals and as the church—the body of Christ? Too busy—too preoccupied—too inwardly focused to even notice the hurting, dying people all around us. The previous chapters of this book addressed the purpose of the church, the fact that God is in charge and that we, as His people, have the privilege of sharing in the power of worship. With that foundation, I now want to discuss the ministry and mission of the church. As disciples, we must broaden the scope of our faith from something that is about us to something that calls us to be about God's purpose in the world.

A Larger Vision

In thinking about this, let's consider: Why do we go to church? Do we go merely to have our needs met or to find comfort for our souls? Do we go in the hopes of finding wisdom and advice for how to handle our current circumstances? In essence, do we go because of what we think we will get out of it, or do we go for a larger reason? Do we love God just for His benefits, or do we grasp the urgency of the gospel that is hope for the hurting and life to the dying? Are we committed to God's purpose, building His Kingdom into the hearts of men and women around the world?

In 1 Thessalonians, Paul addresses a church that is trying to answer some of these same questions. To give you some context for this letter, Paul and Silas were on a missionary journey to the Gentiles (essentially, non-Jews) with the express purpose of spreading the gospel of Jesus Christ. Along the way, they pick up Timothy as they headed to Philippi.

However, in Philippi, everything began to change. People were furious, especially the Jewish people, and they rose up against the outspoken Christians. Paul, Silas, and Timothy were beaten with rods and imprisoned, but that didn't stop them. When they got out of prison, they continued their mission and eventually came to Thessalonica where a great ministry was taking place. Many lives were being changed, yet the Jews became more and more hostile. They threatened not only Paul, Silas and Timothy, but anyone who professed faith in Christ. Thus, in the best interest of the new believers, the three of them left town in the middle of the night, not knowing when or if they would ever return. Pained by having to leave, and by the opposition facing the church, Paul wrote a letter back to the Thessalonian Christians explaining why he came, why he did what he did, and why those actions were honoring to the Lord. Even more so, he reveals in the letter a model for the ministry of the Church of Jesus Christ when it comes to mission.

Paul's letter to the Thessalonians outlines how to achieve and maintain a vital, healthy relationship with God, one lived out in the context of God's family, the Body of Christ. A disciple fully embracing the abundant life promised in Christ is one who takes seriously that he or she has been entrusted with the privilege of sharing the gospel. That privilege is born out through the community of God's people found in His Church. Given its content and hope, the vital church does not view the Gospel as a burden or an inconvenience—but rather a sacred privilege granted by God. It's important to remember the significance of the pain and hardship that Paul had suffered at this point. Why does he continue to endure the beatings and imprisonments and humiliation? He endures them because he knows the weight of what God had asked him to do: "I was delighted, even with all I endured, to come and share the Gospel...." (I Thessalonians 2:8) He considered it a privilege to share the Gospel. He had a vision of his faith in God that transcended his life and encompassed his call to be an instrument of God in the world.

Answering the Call

I find Paul's response very humbling. Think about it. We, as Christians, are called to be ambassadors for Christ. We are asked to make a defense of the Gospel and to share the reason for the hope in our hearts to anyone who will listen. And yet, what is typically our response?

"Do I have to?"

"I don't know that I'm really very good at that..."

"I wouldn't know what to say."

"That would make me feel so uncomfortable."

Can you imagine how that echoes in the ears of our Savior who bled and died to redeem our lives?

Several years ago, the father of one of my best friends, Glenn Baird, died in Chattanooga after a long respiratory illness. Calvin Baird was a great man, a man who served his country on Iwo Jima, a man who became a pillar in Christ's Church. Glenn called me that evening and asked me to come and help lead his father's memorial service. Now, how do you suppose I reacted? Did I say, "Glenn, you know, I have a bunch of things on my calendar and it's inconvenient for me to travel right now. I'm not sure I'm up to it this week." No. To speak at the funeral of my friend's father was a remarkable honor and privilege. I would have happily moved heaven and earth to be there, because I understood what a privilege it was.

The highest honor—the greatest privilege—that our loving Father could bestow upon us is to make us the messengers of the love and grace that has transformed and redeemed our lives in Jesus Christ. There is nothing of more value to Him. He has entrusted us with His truth and asked us to share it with the world. The vital Christian—the vital church - is one that makes the privilege of bearing witness to Christ—in all its forms—the priority of life and ministry; and considers this privilege as a sacred trust rather than a burden.

Further, we will never understand the privilege of what God has entrusted to us until we understand the true nature of the message: we must grasp *the hope and urgency of the Gospel*. Paul writes, "We dared to tell you His Gospel in spite of strong opposition,..." Paul never withered beneath the opposition because he understood the urgency of his task. He clearly understood that apart from Jesus Christ, *there is no life*.

In John 14:6, Jesus said, "I am the way and the truth and the life, no one comes to the Father except through me." If we truly believe that Christ is the Son of God, that He died on the cross and rose on the third day; if we deduce from those facts that Jesus Christ is who He said He was—no less than the Son

of God and the Savior of the world—then His words are true.
If His words are true, then I must accept that the only hope
for me, the only hope for my neighbor, the only hope for the
world is found in that message and I had better get busy trying to share the good news that saved me. How could we do
anything else?

Let's say I have you over for dinner one night. You
come in and find the shelves in my den lined with vials of
medicine. You ask, "What are those?" I answer, "The vials?
They're nothing, really. They have a medicine in them that
is a cure for cancer." How would you respond? Probably
something like, "What are you doing? Are you crazy? Call
the hospital! Call the newspaper! There are people dying
who need that medicine!" In that moment, you would obviously understand the severity of the disease and its devastating impact on people's lives such that you would have an
urgency about sharing such a cure with the world. *The Gospel is nothing less than that*, but until we see it as such, we will
never engage—never be motivated—never truly hunger to
be God's witness, because we simply do not understand the
life-saving nature of the message.

Before he died, Nate Saint, a missionary who was killed
by the Auca Indians even as he served them, wrote:

> *"As we have a high old time this Christmas, may we who
> know Christ hear the cry of the damned as they hurtle
> headlong into the Christless night without ever a chance.
> May we be moved with compassion as our Lord was. May
> we shed tears of repentance for these we have failed to bring
> out of darkness. Beyond the smiling scenes of Bethlehem
> may we see the crushing agony of Golgotha. May God give
> us a new vision of His will concerning the lost and our
> responsibility."* (quoted from the journal of Nate Saint
> in *Through Gates of Splendor*, Elisabeth Elliott)

I have read those words countless times in my ministry,
and every time I do, they wreck me. They wreck me because
I know that I lead my own self-absorbed life, one that often
fails to see those who "hurtle headlong into the Christless
night." This failure must be something that I always keep
before me.

Reclaiming Our Mission

As Christians, our role and responsibility is to share the good news of Christ, but many times we fall short. We just don't get it done. The mission of God lacks urgency for us. Let me ask you: If someone came up to you and said, "I have been thinking a lot about Jesus. Can you explain the Gospel to me? Why do you go to church and why is it so important to you?" Could you answer? And if not, given the stakes, what are you going to do to change that?

A vital, abundant Christian life is one that has an acute awareness of the will of God in regard to those who are lost and a clear understanding of responsibility and call to carry the urgent message of the Gospel to those very people. This, of course, most often happens in the context of the Body. Outreach and mission are the privileges that God grants the church. We are inspired and motivated to share when we realize the significance and urgency of the message, but we also learn that the message is most powerfully shared in the context of relationship. Going back to 1 Thessalonians 2:8, Paul wrote, "we were delighted to share with you not only the gospel of God, but *our lives* as well." (Italics mine.)

Paul's ministry was preaching and teaching, but more than that, he shared his life. He was with the people. He shared his hurts and needs and hopes and prayers—and why? He did so because he understood ministry has far more power, far more relevance, when it is shared in the context of a relationship of mutual love and respect. My old youth pastor used to say, "They'll never care how much you know until they know how much you care." If we are going to be effective servants of Christ, we must be engaged with others. We must invest in their lives with love, and in that context, the Gospel can take root and grow.

That's exactly what happened in my friendship with Scott. The first time I walked into his hospital room, I did not hand him a tract and share the Gospel. I suppose there are times when such an approach might be called for, but the first thing I did was get to know Scott. Scott opened his heart and invited me in because he knew I cared about him regardless of his illness or prior life choices. In the context of relationship, I was freed to share the Gospel and Scott was able to listen.

While we may recognize the truth of God's call in this regard, we are still reluctant to do it. We'll share the Gospel—we'll share some Scripture we memorized and maybe even get our hands dirty serving food or digging wells—but don't ask us to share ourselves. If we did that, then others might find out that we're not perfect—that we have struggles—that we don't have all the answers and that our lives don't match up to the image we project. Somewhere along the line, Christians started believing that if they allowed others to see their struggles, it might lessen their ability to witness effectively. Let me tell you right now: such an idea is completely ridiculous. In fact, nothing could be further from the truth. It is through your struggles that your witness has power! It is through your weakness that Christ's strength is made manifest!

I'll let you in on a little secret: I know you're not perfect. No, I have not read your mail or filled your house with surveillance equipment. I don't have to. I know. Further, I will assume you know that I am not perfect, either. Trust me, no one is going to pass out from shock when they find this out about you. This "revelation" will not surprise anyone. They already know! No one is perfect. Isn't that why we go to church, because we realize that we need someone outside of us to save us? You bet. So, let's get this over with once and for all and get on to the business of ministry. We don't have to be perfect to invest and share our lives with others.

In 2 Corinthians 4:7, Paul writes, "We have this treasure in jars of clay to show that this all-surpassing power is from God and not from us." We're not perfect. We are all fellow travelers on the same journey, and Paul said we need to walk that road together.

We live in a rapidly changing world among people whom scholars tell us are far less concerned with pithy arguments and well-crafted speeches, and far more concerned with simply seeing truth lived out. They want to see truth in the context of human relationships, and friends, we have been charged by God to share His truth. While it may challenge us and push us beyond our comfort zones, I can also tell you that it is one of the great joys in the Christian life to sense that you are being used as His instrument in the life of another. There is no better feeling. I close with the words of a poem by Sam Shoemaker, *So I Stay Near The Door*:

"I stay near the door.

The door is the most important door in the world—it is the door through which men walk when they find God. There's no use my going way inside, and staying there, when so many are still outside, and they, as much as I, crave to know where the door is.

And all that so many ever find
Is only a wall where a door ought to be.

They creep along the wall like blind men, with outstretched, groping hands,

Feeling for a door, knowing there must be a door,
Yet they never find it...so I stay near the door.

The most important thing that any person can do is to take hold of one of those blind, groping hands and to put it on the latch—that latch that only clicks and opens to that person's own touch. Men die outside that door, as starving beggars die, on cold nights in cruel cities in the dead of winter—die for want of what is within their grasp. Nothing else matters compared to helping them find it, so I stay near the door."

Scott was one of those people. He was one of those blind, groping hands, feeling for a door, knowing there must be a door, but always unable to find it. God allowed me the privilege of putting his hand on the latch of the door to the Kingdom that clicked at his touch. Consider today who might be walking past you each day, groping for the door, blind, and unable to find it. Do you see them? Do you care?

Abundant, vital Christian living comes when we engage in a life beyond ourselves, a life committed to the larger plan and purpose of God. When we understand the urgency of the gospel and live out our call to share it, life becomes rich and deep and meaningful. In being about what God is about, we find the life we have been looking for all along. So go, stand by the door.

8

"Be kind and compassionate to one another, forgiving each other, just as in Christ God forgave you."

EPHESIANS 4:32

"If you cannot free people from their wrongs and see them as the needy people they are, you enslave yourself to your own painful past, and by fastening yourself to the past, you let your hate become your future. You can reverse your future only by releasing other people from their pasts. You will know when you have done this when you can recall those who hurt you and feel the power to wish them well."

LEWIS SMEDES, *FORGIVE AND FORGET*

A number of years ago, I had an experience that taught me a lot about myself, and like so many other times, I had to learn it the hard way. I wish I could learn to take God at His word and simply do what He says instead of always having to be taught in the "crucibles" of life. I was working as an associate pastor at a church in Chattanooga, Tennessee, ministering to youth and their families and overseeing a number of staff in relationship to those ministries. As can sometimes be the case, one of my direct reports, responsible for a vital element of our ministry, was not performing well. She was a delightful human being, gifted in many ways, but circumstances were such that she was not able to manage the details. I took steps to meet with her, providing direction and setting goals and expectations. Things would improve for a time, but then revert back. Naturally, I brought my concerns to the personnel committee of our church. We followed the necessary steps, creating a process for improvement with benchmarks and timing for completion. Even so, it was clear to me and everyone involved that we needed to make a change. We did not want to lose her, but we did want to provide more leadership and direction, so we appointed a new person as a "co-leader" with her.

I knew she would see this as a demotion and take it very hard. There is nothing worse than having to let someone go or to tell them, in spite of their best efforts, that changes have to be made. To make matters worse, she was a member of our church, a person whom I had come to love and care for, a person whose family I valued and adored. As a result, I was miserable. I knew the day and time we were going to meet, and the preceding days were awful. My stomach hurt. I could not eat. I could not sleep. I knew it was the right decision for the overall ministry of the church, but the anticipation of having the actual conversation was killing me.

The day finally came. She sat down in my office, probably suspecting what was next, but not knowing for sure. We traded small talk for a few minutes but I couldn't take the tension any longer, and the words just came tumbling out. Stammering and stuttering, I tried to be as gentle as possible. Surprisingly, she seemed to take it well. She paused a moment, then said she understood what was happening and why and that she felt we would be able to move forward in a healthy, positive fashion.

Whew! I was so relieved. When she left my office, I felt as if a huge weight had been lifted off my shoulders. Unfortunately, that feeling didn't last long. Later that afternoon, the woman's husband called me and berated me for what I had done. I was doing everything I could to maintain my composure, but in the face of his relentless verbal attacks, I snapped. I raised my voice and fought back. Yes, indeed, the thin veneer of my Christian faith slid right off and I tore into him. "If you got a bad review in your job, do you think it would be appropriate for your wife to go down and talk to your boss?" In my opinion, it was not his place to engage the situation. Telling him that, of course, was like pouring gasoline on a fire. Truth be told, that was what I wanted. My sinful nature wanted to light him up. And, I did.

In fact, I made him so mad he went straight to my boss, the Senior Pastor of the church. Within a few hours of my phone call with the husband, I was summoned to the Senior Pastor's office—pronto. (That's Texan for immediately!) When I walked in, I was face to face with the husband—still fuming, steam nearly visible from his ears, face red, eyes boring a hole right through me. He proceeded to dress me down again and demanded that I apologize. He further suggested that the Senior Pastor restore his wife's position. I was livid. Who did he think he was, calling for an apology! Right then, I started asking the Lord for permission to clock this guy! I would have given anything in that moment to have *not* worked at a church. Thankfully, the Senior Pastor stepped in and we were both sent home. While the decision may have been right, my behavior was certainly wrong.

Even so, I couldn't let it go and later that evening, I was still enraged. My heart was racing. My face was red. My wife took one look at me and said, "What is going on?" I couldn't even talk. I started pacing. Finally, at 11 o'clock that night, I got a hammer and took out my frustration on a huge oak tree at the end of our driveway. I hit that tree so hard and for so long that the head of the hammer broke off and went flying across our neighbor's yard into the darkness. Not satisfied, I went back to the garage for a bigger weapon—a sledgehammer. After twenty minutes, drenched in sweat, my hands aching from blisters, I had finally had enough. I went back in the house, exhausted. That night became known as "tree night," and to this day, that tree still stands, filled with dents and pock marks as a lasting memorial to my anger.

Healing the Hurt

I bet, at some point, maybe even recently, you have felt exactly as I did that day—wounded, angry, attacked, and hurt. Someone did something to you, hurting you in a deep and profound way. They did something you never thought any human being on the planet would ever do to you. And you were enraged. You told your story of injustice to others, and at hearing the news, they, too, were angry right along with you. You felt justified. You had a *right* to be angry.

In those moments, what did you do? You stewed. You obsessed. You got in bed at night and your anger crowded out any other thoughts. You played out imaginary conversations with the offending party where you were severe and sarcastic and always had a perfect comeback. When you woke in the morning, you thought about what you would do if you saw the person—what you would say—how you would respond. You thought about the things that should happen to that person if God had any sense of justice at all. Truth be told, you sort of liked the feeling. It gave you a sense of power. Someone had done you wrong and you reveled, just a bit, in your righteous anger because it took away the pain of the wound, even if only for a moment.

The problem with such thinking is we cannot possibly sustain such feelings and live a healthy life. It is far too consuming. Anger will eventually destroy us if we make no effort to forgive and tend to our wounds. If all we do is relive the disappointments in our lives and express our anger about them, we will never actually move forward into the life that God is calling us to live. We must summon the courage to honestly face our wounds, the people or circumstances, which created them, and the feelings which result. Thankfully, we don't have to do it alone. The Great Physician, expertly skilled in healing the wounds of the human heart, is available to us whenever we call on Him.

 There are times when it can be extremely hard to read certain parts of the Bible, because God may show us something we don't want to see or deal with. I hate it when that happens, moments when God shows me that I am full of myself. You know the sort of passages I'm talking about: loving your enemies, praying for those who persecute you, thinking about others first, giving away your money. Sometimes, I just want to close the book and pretend it doesn't exist. There are times when I simply feel like I cannot do what God is asking of me. No way.

Ephesians 4:29 is a classic example: "Do not let any unwholesome talk come out of your mouths, but only what is helpful for building others up according to their needs, that it may benefit those who listen." Easier said than done, but regardless of how much we may want to ignore it, it's still the truth. When we live in truth, God has the opportunity to carve away the dead and lifeless parts of our hearts and heal us.

In Ephesians 4, Paul is discussing this notion of anger and malice that we often feel in response to being hurt. He goes on in verse 31 to say, "Get rid of all bitterness, rage and anger, brawling and slander, along with every form of malice." Interestingly, the Greek word for "get rid of" allows no room for delay. It's not something you should think about or carefully consider. You are just supposed to do it. It's sort of like the way you feel when you open up a carton of rotten milk. You don't stand around and breathe in its fragrance, thinking, "Hmm, I wonder what I should do?" No! You instantly pour it down the sink and do whatever is necessary to get that stench out or your refrigerator and out of your life.

Even so, I've noticed that when we're angry or when we've been wronged, we don't want to get rid of our anger. Andy Stanley, pastor of Northpoint Church in Atlanta, put it this way: "How insensitive it is of Paul, speaking from 2,000 years ago, knowing nothing of my life or circumstances, to tell me to get rid of my anger. Like he knows!" I love it. That's how I feel.

The truth of the matter is that we take our wounds and disappointments, and the corresponding anger we feel, and we make friends with them. There's an almost prideful ownership we take in our pain. We cling to it. We protect it as if it is something of great value to us. The mere suggestion that we should let it go, well, that's clearly coming from someone who doesn't understand what we've been through. If they knew what happened, how bad it was, surely they would be angry right alongside us! It's hard to fathom, but we can become comfortable in our "woundedness" such that we unintentionally prevent healing. The wound and pain is what we know, so we stay with it. To live without it seems unsettling somehow.

Does Paul have a right to admonish our bitterness and anger? Well, let's think about that. He's not writing from a beach in Hawaii. He is writing from prison. He is in a deplorable situation. His friends and advocates are scared of persecution so they don't do anything. He's alone. Do you think Paul had a right to harbor malice and anger in his heart? Did he have something to be genuinely upset about? You bet he did, and still, he writes, "Get rid of all anger…" Amazing. If you put me in the same situation, I'm fairly certain that is not what I would write.

Taking a step back, when you consider his whole letter to the Ephesians, the theme is unity. Paul wanted to help this church become a vital, healthy community of believers. With that in mind, he knew that if people couldn't let go of their anger, they could never be whole, as individuals or as a body of believers. I think God was teaching Paul the same lessons, and the Ephesians were benefitting from the wisdom of Paul's experience. I believe he prayerfully considered how God wanted him to respond to his own circumstances, so he

p 125 forgive ourselves

forgave his captors and focused on God's presence and forgiveness. Perhaps, we should do the same.

Vital Medicine

In this life make no mistake: we will be wounded. However, there is a remedy—a cure—that can bring us the healing we so desperately need. That cure is *forgiveness*. Like it or not, the answer is forgiveness. A person who is experiencing the abundant life promised in Jesus Christ is one marked by a spiritual maturity in being able to forgive others. Consequently, when churches are filled by disciples who learn this, those churches become forgiving communities. Instead of shooting their wounded, as churches so often do, they become communities of grace, repentance, and restoration.

In the New Testament, there are two Greek words used for forgiveness. One has to do with court imagery—a judge who pardons a guilty person. The second is more relational. The second implies that forgiveness is an experience to be shared between two people, offered by one to the other. It is the second word that Paul uses in Ephesians 4. We are to be a body of believers, a community, continually going to each other in love and offering forgiveness.

Let's think about what that means, practically. As a believer in Christ, I will offer forgiveness to whoever has wronged me. They may not recognize they need it. They may not even want it. Even so, I will choose to get rid of the anger and bitterness that is infecting my own life and allow my own wounds to heal by forgiving. Thus, relationships are restored and subsequently, Christ is reflected to the world. If the Church—the body of Christ—is ever going to be unified there must be a vehicle for restoration and healing, a remedy for the wounds of life. There is, and that remedy is forgiveness.

I am married to a wonderful woman. Like all good men, I married way above me. In my own church, I am known as Leigh Swanson's husband. I'm not kidding. I still can't figure out how I got her to marry me. It was obviously an act of God. You may find this shocking, but, in my marriage to Leigh, I have made some mistakes. Let me rephrase that: I have made some *serious* mistakes. In fact, one time, in a fit of complete irrationality, I told Leigh that she was not really contributing enough to the management of our household. Big mistake. Huge. Now, to my credit, I am generally pretty good at knowing when I have messed up, and when I do, I admit it. I grovel. Some groveling involves flowers, other times a card or jewelry—and one time, as the result of a particularly monumental error, groveling meant a piece of furniture. I groveled and gave her a leather chair and ottoman, as I recall. However, here's the thing: none of my offerings resulted in a restored relationship. Regardless of my attempts to fix the problem, the relationship was not restored until Leigh chose to grant me forgiveness. She could have easily accepted my gifts and still not forgiven me. Thankfully, that is not the heart of my wife. Instead, she accepted *and* she forgave.

The same is true in the life of the church. Friends, we are all flawed, fallen people. It is ridiculous to think that just because we all love God that we are never going to do anything to offend or hurt each other. So, if that's true, then what is the only thing that is going to keep the body of Christ moving forward in a God-honoring way? Forgiveness. Without it, we're stuck. With it, we have a chance to be a true community that reflects Christ to the world.

A Tough Assignment

I am under no illusions. I recognize that forgiveness is tough. I can understand, in a cerebral way, that I need to forgive and still not feel like it. Thankfully, Paul thought of everything. He addresses our *motivation* to forgive. The second half of verse 32 says, "....forgiving each other, just as in Christ, God forgave you." We can't really argue with that one. This is the key to the entire theological doctrine of forgiveness. Forgiveness has nothing to do with the other person. Your ability to forgive is not based on their worth, it is not based on a change in their character, the quality of their confession, nor the amount of pain they caused you. The ability to forgive is based on how God treated us. Jesus states the connection rather clearly in the Lord's Prayer, "Forgive us our debts as we forgive our debtors."

This is where it becomes vitally important that we understand the nature of sin. Based on the quality of my life, I know I can never earn the glory of God's heaven. I am a mess. In the face of my ongoing and pervasive sin, God sent His son to die, so that I could live. The punishment that should have been on me was on Him. I know that, and for that, I am eternally grateful. That said, think about your own life.

Think about all the times you told God you would never do it again. Think about how He welcomed you back with open arms when you did. We've all been the prodigal—taking and squandering our Father's things and slinking back in shame. I don't know about you, but I've always returned to a Father excited to welcome me back into His family. Now, if God gave us the gift of forgiveness, then who are we to deny it to others? At the foot of the cross, we lose our right to withhold forgiveness from anyone else.

James Dobson tells the story of South African police officer James Van De Broek. During apartheid, Van De Broek did many things in the name of justice. Before a court of law, he acknowledged his role in the killing of an 18-year-old boy, shooting him at point blank range and then burning his body to ashes. Eight years later, he returned to the same house and seized the boy's father. He proceeded to pour gasoline over his body and light him on fire, forcing the man's wife to watch. The last words his wife heard her husband utter were, "Forgive them." When the South African Truth and Reconciliation Commission asked the woman what she hoped would happen to Van De Broek, she said, "I want three things. I want Mr. Van De Broek to take me to the place where they burned my husband's body so that I can gather the dust and bury him properly. Second, he took my family from me and I still have a great deal of love to give. So, twice a month, I would like for him to come to the ghetto and spend a day with me so I can be a mother to him. Third, I would like him to know that he is forgiven by God and that I forgive him too. I would like someone to lead me to where he is seated, so I can embrace him and he can know my forgiveness is real." As the court officer came to lead the woman across the courtroom, Van De Broek fainted in his seat, overwhelmed by the grace and love being extended to him. At that moment, the courtroom burst into a chorus of Amazing Grace.

Do you see the spiritual power that can be unleashed through forgiveness? If we are honest, often times, we are holding others hostage for things they are not capable of giving us. Someone hurts us, and we refuse to forgive, until what? What are we waiting for? What do we think is going to happen? Your father can never give you the childhood you wish you had. Your boss will never be able to erase the emotional baggage he drudged up when you were let go. The world cannot take away your child's diagnosis. The drunk driver will never be able to go back in time and call a cab. If you can never be repaid, then why not cancel the debt? By not forgiving, you bind yourself to the past.

The late Lewis Smedes, a longtime professor at Fuller Theological Seminary, wrote what I believe to be the best book ever written on forgiveness entitled, *Forgive and Forget.* In it, he writes:

> *"If you cannot free people from their wrongs and see them as the needy people they are, you enslave yourself to your own painful past, and by fastening yourself to the past, you let your hate become your future. You can reverse your future only be releasing other people from their pasts. You will know when you have done this when you can recall those who hurt you and feel the power to wish them well."*

Why not unleash the power of God to set you free from the burden and actually bear witness to Christ's love in the world? It is the most powerful thing a Christian can do! As Andy Stanley put it, "Forgiveness is the number one export of the Church." Our core message is that God forgives, so shouldn't that be what we are primarily known for? Aren't we those who claim to be forgiven people? How incongruous and hypocritical it would be for a forgiven people, bearing a message of forgiveness, to fail to be forgiving. This is our responsibility in Christ. This is our calling. If you have been forgiven, then you are charged to offer the gift to others. If you find it impossible to offer to others, then I believe you need to spend more time in contemplating the nature and state of your own heart.

We will only be able to forgive when we see people in light of the cross. When we realize how much we need the grace of God—when we understand what we are capable of—only then can we accept others in the same vein. We must face the fact that we have been wounded, but we have also wounded others, many times in fact. My prayer is that you will be able to mature as a disciple of Jesus Christ—to get rid of your anger and let go of your wounds—and in so doing, release others from your past so that you can embrace God's future for your life.

Prayer is a critical part of this. When others have wronged me and I have held tight to my anger, it is often only through prayer that I have been able to see them at the foot of the cross. Prayer is a discipline that God uses in our lives so that we see with His eyes. If you find yourself struggling to forgive someone, pray for them. It'll change you.

What Forgiveness Is Not

I know that you may still be balking at this idea. Perhaps there is something about it that does not feel right, almost as if something is missing. Yes, I believe forgiveness is a vital part of an abundant Christian life, but let me also be clear about what forgiveness is not. Forgiveness is not pretending that something did not happen. Forgiveness is not blind acceptance of another, regardless of destructive behavior. Yes, we need to forgive, but that does not mean we naively put ourselves back in the situation that hurt us to begin with. It does not mean that actions have no consequences. If someone wrongs you, there may be social or civil consequences for those wrongs. I can forgive someone for vandalizing my front yard, but they should still pay for the damage. I can forgive my boss for verbally abusing me, but I will still look for another job. I can forgive someone for breaking into my home, but I can still allow the system of justice to play out appropriately. Forgiveness is a powerful tool for healing, but it does not require us to become a doormat.

Further, forgiveness is not giving up on justice. On some level, we think God's command to forgive is somehow unfair to us, because it feels like the person who wronged us is "getting away" with something. That is *not* the case. Forgiveness is, in fact, congruent with God's justice. Our sinful actions and the way we wound others must be answered. Were that not true, then Jesus Christ would never have died for us. God would have winked at our sin and said, "Never mind. I love you no matter what you do." He does love us, but our sin has to be addressed and His love comes at a price. God is just, and He will judge the actions of all people, including those who hurt us. This is freeing news for us. It frees us because we are not capable of mitigating justice. This truth frees us from trying. Is there anyone who could look at the actions of another and truly judge what is a just and right consequence? I know I can't, and I certainly don't want to have to be in that position.

Praise God, He frees me from the responsibility and burden of judgment. I don't have to lose sleep over it. Sure, we can waste all kinds of energy imagining what a person deserves or what we hope happens to them. I suppose it is a natural part of our sinful nature, but it is unhealthy and God wants to free us from that. We don't have to worry about what we'll say when we see them or how we'll get them back, because God will take this burden from us. Forgiveness is not pretending nothing happened, it is trusting God when it does happen. It's believing that part of God's holy, eternal nature is perfect justice. Sin does get answered, so we can let go of what has been done to us. God is going to handle it. It is another measure of God's grace.

The Hardest Part

Finally, I think the hardest part of forgiving is forgiving yourself. I believe, for many of us, this is the part we struggle with most. It doesn't make logical sense, but nothing about forgiveness is logical. God reminds us in Jeremiah 31:34, "I will forgive their iniquities and remember their sins no more." He tells us again in 2 Corinthians 5:21, "...in Christ, we might become the righteousness of God." God's love for us is so deep, so vast, so immeasurable, that He sacrificed His Son to atone for our sins. Through that death, we are cleansed and forgiven. The debt was paid and we have a clean slate. Jesus said on the cross, "It is finished." The work is complete. Over. Done.

But often, even when we accept that we need to forgive others, it is hard to believe that God will really forgive us. We know too much about the darkness of our own hearts to accept that God's grace could cover it. We refuse to believe what God says in Romans 5:20, "Where sin increased, grace increased all the more." We refuse to forgive ourselves. The fact of the matter is we cannot out-sin God's grace. It is not possible. God forgives us and yet, we cannot forgive ourselves. Maybe this little story will help. It has sure helped me.

The Picnic

Bob Benson is the author and it's called "Sunday School Picnic." Perhaps we can all learn to live this way.

"Do you remember when they used to have old-fashioned Sunday School picnics? It was before air-conditioning. They said, 'We'll meet at Sycamore Lodge in Shelby Park on Saturday at 4:30. You bring your supper and we'll furnish the tea.' So you planned to go, but at the last minute when you went to make your supper, all you could find in your refrigerator was one dried up piece of bologna and just enough mustard in the bottom of the jar so that you got it all over your knuckles trying to get it out. So you made your sandwich, stuck it in a bag, and went to the picnic.

When it came time to eat, you sat at the end of the table and spread out your sandwich, but the folks next to you—that lady was a good cook and she had worked all day—fried chicken, baked beans and potato salad— homemade rolls, sliced tomatoes, pickles and celery— and she topped it off with two chocolate pies. And they spread it all out beside you—and there you were with your baloney sandwich. But they said to you, 'Why don't we just put it all together? Come on—there's plenty of chicken and plenty of pie—and we just love baloney sandwiches—let's just put it all together!' But you said, half embarrassed, 'Oh no—really—I'm fine.' She insisted, though, and so there you sat eating like a king when you came like a pauper."

Isn't that just like us? I see so many people running through life hanging on to their sad little baloney sandwich, essentially saying, "Oh no—God's not going to get my sandwich. No sir—this is mine!" Did you ever see anyone like that—so needy—just about half-starved to death—hanging on to their sorry baloney sandwich for dear life? The King has laid out a feast for us, a banquet of love and forgiveness, but we refuse to eat it. Instead, there we sit, hanging on to our sandwich. It's ridiculous. *He doesn't need your sandwich. You need His chicken.* Toss the baloney. Eat the feast. He loves you and He forgives you, so it's time. It's time. Let go. Partake of the feast!

You and I are messed up and we are going to hurt each other. And if that's true, and we can't forgive, then we'll never experience the glory of the body of Christ. However, if we can learn the gift of forgiveness, born in the honest admission of our own sin, then God can use us for His good, beyond anything we could create or imagine. I pray that we will become vital, forgiving people and a vital, forgiving Church.

9

*"The body is a unit, though it is made up of many
parts; and though all its parts are many, they form
one body. So it is with Christ…"*

1 CORINTHIANS 12:12

*"(A Christian's) conversion and renewal is not,
therefore, an end in itself, as it has often been in-
terpreted and represented in a far too egocentric
Christianity. When we convert and are renewed
in the totality of our being, we cross the thresh-
old of our private existence and move out into
the open…"*

KARL BARTH, *CHURCH DOGMATICS*

I am a beach person. Some people are mountain people, but
I am a beach person. I love the sound of the waves, their
gentle, relentless rhythm lapping at the shoreline. I love the
shells and the birds and the way the sun can light the sky
ablaze as she sets. It feels as if I am somehow closer to God
when I am at the beach. As such, many years ago, when I
began taking an annual study leave, I tried to find a way to
spend those days at the beach.

In my current church, I am blessed by several families
who allow me the use of their beachfront condos for this
purpose, and this past spring was no different. I joyfully set
off for a week of study and reflection at New Smyrna Beach.
Because this time is so critical to my entire year, I work very
hard preparing in order to make the most of every moment.
I had carefully planned the books I wanted to read, the sub-
jects I wanted to explore, the Scriptures I would study. I had
methodically scheduled each day: time for morning prayer
and journaling, time for walks and reflection, time for meals,
time for sleep. I had gone to the grocery store and bought
everything I would need. I had thought of every possible
detail, except I could not have anticipated that New Smyrna

Beach would experience record amounts of rainfall during my visit. In a four-day period, the area received more than 21 inches of rain, and let me tell you, I think I saw every drop. From the moment I arrived on a Monday morning, it never stopped raining. Ever.

Now, initially, I thought, "That's fine. I don't need to be outside anyway. I can just hunker down and get more work done." It seemed to be a great plan, and it was—for awhile. On the afternoon of my second day, I realized that I had not seen another human being in nearly 48 hours. As an extrovert, that was kind of tough for me. I need people, but there was simply no one around. And trust me, I tried to find them. There was just no one there. From the balcony of the condo I was using, I could see up and down the beach. Every 45 minutes or so, I would go out and look in each direction. No one ever walked by. Not a soul. By the third day, I was starting to feel a little paranoid, so I decided to brave the rain and go for a walk. I was looking in the buildings on either side of mine, looking for lights, for any sign of movement or life. It was like the entire area had been evacuated. It crossed my mind that perhaps Jesus had returned and I had been left behind.

As that day wore on, I could not shake the feeling that I was the only person alive on the planet. Intellectually, I knew that was not true. I knew someone had to be out there, but I could not see them. Finally, on the fourth day, feeling completely isolated and cut-off from civilization, I decided I needed to see a newspaper. I got in my car and set off for the nearest convenience store. As I inched along, the water had risen so high that authorities had shut the roads down to one passable lane. Cars had to take turns travelling in each direction, and as I waited my turn, I wondered if my car could even make it through all the water. In that moment, I made a decision. I was done. I was lonely and missing my family. I determined on the spot that I was not going to get rained in for the rest of the weekend. I turned around, went back to the condo, packed up my things and got off the island before the roads shut down completely. You cannot imagine the sense of relief I felt when I walked back into my house and was greeted by my wife and children, even if I did look like a drowned rat.

Reconnecting

Thankfully for me, reconnecting into community was easy because my family was happy to have me back, but I believe my experience is becoming more and more the story of our lives. We are becoming more and more isolated from one another.

Recent George Gallup research on American isolationism supports this idea. Gallup writes, "We are physically detached from each other. We change places of residence frequently. One survey revealed that seven in ten people do not know their neighbors. As many as one-third of Americans admit to frequent periods of loneliness." As our culture becomes more focused on individualism, we become more self-absorbed and less interested in the concept of "others." We want things our way, in our order, in our time and at our convenience. Nothing has inherent value, but we value things—and others—only insofar as they are able to add something to our lives. Our view of others is utilitarian in nature. Coupled with the explosion of technologies that allow us to communicate without ever being in the presence of another person—texting, instant messaging, social networking—isolation seems inevitable. It is disturbing to me that my teenage children communicate almost exclusively through text messaging. I find students today are not nearly as comfortable or equipped to engage adults in conversation. They have no experience engaging in-person with their peers, let alone with adults. While we may love the convenience and speed of technology, there are consequences, many of which we are just beginning to understand.

While hard to quantify, it is a feeling; we might not acknowledge it intellectually, but on some level we feel like I did on the beach—oddly separate, disconnected, alone. As a result, I think people are looking for ways to interact. In a recent *New York Times* article, Deborah Schonemen described the growing yoga craze in Southern California, "More than a grueling workout, Mr. Marino's class is a community...students go almost daily to keep fit, as well as for the social life. They bond...." Even more revealing was a statement from one student, "I feel euphoric after. Yoga people on the whole are super cool and everyone is there to work on their own thing." People are obviously desperate for community, but even when they find it, it's still about them. The concept of community for the sake of the individual is a contradiction in and of itself. What a sham.

Flash mobs are another recent cultural phenomenon. A flash mob is a random group of people who gather on short notice around a single idea or purpose. For instance, when Michael Jackson died, a flash mob swelled in the center of London to dance to Michael Jackson's music. No one knew each other, but there was comfort in numbers, in other people with common interests and passions. In modern communities such as these, even when people are together, they are still alone.

Can these sorts of communities, the communities of our current culture, sustain us in our pain, lift us up in our weakness, rejoice with us in our discoveries, or hold us accountable to our core values? Can these communities provide an enduring place of grace and love, as well as honesty and truth? In my opinion, the answer is no. They can't. Without a higher purpose, these communities are centered on individual needs. And if that's the case, where does that leave us? Living in a divided, chaotic, fast-paced, isolated world, where can we find authentic community? How can we find answers to the nagging, somewhat neurotic sense of loneliness and detachment we feel?

Life Together

The answer, of course, is Christian community as described by Paul in his first letter to the Corinthians. Paul is writing to the Corinthian church about a number of issues, not the least of which was trying to understand what it meant to be a "body." Corinth was a bustling city of commerce, a melting pot of cultures, full of people eager to create their fortunes. As the Holy Spirit grew the church there, the people who had flocked to its community were unique and diverse and drawn together through a common faith. What did God want for them in terms of the community? How could they live together? I believe these are the same questions we face today as the church has literally become a global community.

In his book, *Life Together*, Dietrich Bonhoeffer wrote, "Life together under the word will remain sound and healthy only where it does not form itself into a movement, an order, a society…but rather where it understands itself as being part of the one, holy, catholic Christian church, where it shares, actively and passively, in the sufferings and struggles of the whole church." For Bonhoeffer, the ability of the Christian community to live together was based solely on God's word—being under the word, guided by the word, grounded in the word. Further, he wisely taught that our ability to live together is based on our understanding of the larger whole, not merely our own individual needs or desires.

Paul's instruction in 1 Corinthians 12 illuminates for us this idea of community. It begins with the idea that everyone is gifted, "Now to each one, the manifestation of the Spirit is given for the common good." Essentially, Paul is saying that everyone has value and purpose; every member of the body is important. If God has given each of us gifts and He wants us to use them for His glory, we are purposed and valuable in Christian community—in the body of Christ.

This past year, my two sons played basketball for Winter Park High School and their team won the Florida 6A State Championship. What was unique about the team was the way they came together over the course of the season. They actually lost their first game, but over time, they grew as a team. Each player had a role to play, and while those roles evolved, eventually each one became comfortable in their role. Everyone made a contribution. Some had larger roles than others, but each role was important, and all the players recognized that without the contributions of each player, their team was not nearly as good. Everyone on that team was needed and valued. We need to have that same understanding in the community of faith. No one is unimportant. Everyone is valued. Everyone has a vital role to play in God's Kingdom, and if they don't play their role, our "team" suffers.

Far too often, I encounter people with no confidence in themselves. On some level, subconscious even, they do not believe they have gifts worthy of sharing or being used within the body of Christ. Consequently, the body limps along, impaired by an absence of gifts. It's like being all suited up for the game, but when the coach calls your name, you chose to stay on the bench. Get in the game! Your team needs you! Brennan Manning wrote of this tendency in *Abba's Child*, saying, "We judge ourselves unworthy servants, and that judgment becomes a self-fulfilling prophecy. We deem ourselves too inconsiderable to be used even by a God capable of miracles with no more than mud and spit. And thus our false humility shackles an otherwise omnipotent God."

Uh-oh. You probably didn't think of that, did you? Our continued negativity about our gifts and ability in the Kingdom actually shackles the omnipotent God! May it never be! If you don't know what your gifts are, pray that God will reveal them; work to refine and grow them. But more importantly— offer them—use them. The Church is not always very good at helping us identify and apply our gifts, but that is no excuse. Keep searching. Plug into a community and contribute.

You're In, Not Out

Your unique role in the community is significant because God has made the community significant. For now, the community of faith is His Kingdom on earth. We—the body of Christ—are the incarnation of Jesus Christ on earth. Christ was the incarnation of God. The Church is the incarnation of Jesus to the world. We are His earthly, living body. We are His hands and feet.

The physical image of a body could mean many different things, but in 1 Corinthians, Paul is focused on the body as a unified whole. The body is one unit and all of us who profess faith are a part of that entity. We are not detached—we are connected. We are not isolated—we are joined. We so desperately want to be part of something that makes our lives meaningful, and God has given us that opportunity. You're not out, you're in! His desire for us is to live together. We are all part of something bigger than ourselves, and we have a role to play, a role only we can fill. If our God, revealed to us as Father, Son and Holy Spirit, is a relational being, one God in three persons, then as His earthly body, we too, are relational and designed to live in unity. Humbling, isn't it?

It is important to remember that while our call to community is from God, there is no guarantee that His community will function perfectly. In many ways, this is the hard part. Have you ever gone to a big family reunion and wondered, "How am I related to these people? How is this even possible? I don't even *like* these people!" Believe it or not, someone probably thought the same thing about you! The body of Christ is no different.

In an editorial for *Leadership Journal*, Kevin Miller wrote, "An ordinary church... lacks vision, or more commonly, has a vision, but has no idea how to achieve it. There are frequent miscommunications and misinformation arising from pride or people simply not reading the bulletin. Traditions have outlived their usefulness, but people still feel attached to them, and there are never enough Sunday School teachers. Did I mention there's rarely enough parking, or money, or facilities to make things work?" It's true. Our communities are far from perfect. Most of us attend ordinary churches full of ordinary people. We're just people—sinful, fallen, frail people. That's why we're in church, right? Because we know we are sinful and need a savior.

Even so, there is something in many of us that still whispers, "It's the Church. The Church is supposed to do things right and never let me down." When we have unrealistic expectations, we end up disappointed and reluctant to engage, and in so doing, the body of Christ suffers. I am the pastor of a church and I can assure you that my staff and I work very hard—and sometimes, we fail. Much as I try to avoid it, failure is still a regular part of my life. I'm human.

In his book, *Love One Another*, Gerald Sittser wrote, "When the church is functioning at her best, there is simply no community on earth that can rival it. But when the church is functioning at her worst, there is no community on earth that can do as much damage." I have certainly seen both sides of this truth. Nothing warms my heart more than watching our church rally around someone in crisis or comfort someone through grief. However, nothing is more painful than watching the fallout of sin and poor decisions infect our church family.

The church will fail you. If she hasn't, she will. Therefore, if you disengage every time a person in the church makes a mistake, you will never live in community. The church is full of flawed people. That is why Paul says we all have the same Spirit—because we all need the same Spirit—the Spirit of love and grace and forgiveness.

This is true in individual churches, but also in the broader context, in the Church of Jesus Christ. I hear people complain about the "institutional" church—theological controversies, moral failures, questionable spending, bureaucratically slow processes—and they say, "Well, I don't want to be a part of that. I want to do church my way." I firmly believe that God has called the church to be a global community. And if that is the case, it requires getting a large group of sinful people to work together, which is not going to happen without some bumps along the way. Withdrawing from the church because of its institutional faults is like being an elbow and saying, "This body is falling apart! The heart and lungs are weak; there is too much flab around the middle. I'm just going to go it alone." What possible good does that do? An elbow apart from the body is of no use whatsoever.

Now, to be sure, we need to find a good fit. We need to find a Christian church that feels like home—a place where we can connect and use our gifts. However, we cannot expect perfection. Once we find a community and engage amidst fellow sinners, we must pray that God will use us. God has appointed the Church to be His earthly body—His earthly community—and regardless of its flaws, we were designed to be part of this body, to reflect God's love and grace to the world around us. Imperfect—yes. Impotent—no.

Community As Witness

Finally, we need to understand the way in which we are a community is an essential part of our witness to the world. That's why God brings us together, why we are baptized into one body. In *The Connecting Church*, Randy Frazee says, "In a culture of individualism, when do non-Christians get to see other Christians loving each other in such a way that it compels them to run to Jesus Christ? The church has often mirrored the culture by making Christianity an individual sport."

We have, haven't we? We have put so much emphasis on being in Bible studies and support groups and other ministries so that we can grow, we have unintentionally fostered spiritual individualism that is not part of God's design.

The evangelical church has created a multitude of ways to make my faith stronger, my outlook better, and my peace greater. As a result, I go to church for me, and I forget to consider the role God intended for me, serving the larger body. It's that sort of individualistic thinking that leads to rapid departures. We don't like something, so we withdraw. Withdrawing says it's all about me and what I want and need. It is a symptom of our increasingly isolated society. The reality is that God has called you to be in community. It's not about you, but rather, the point is to live out God's plan and purpose for your life through His earthly body, the Church.

In his book, *The Great Evangelical Disaster*, the late Francis Schaeffer wrote:

> *"Our relationship with each other is the criterion the world uses to judge whether our message is truthful—Christian community is the final apologetic."*

Wow. This makes me wonder, if a non-believer came and observed your church—the way you interact, the way you love each other, the way you serve one another, the way you worship together—would that experience cause them to run to Jesus Christ or away from Him?

I want us to learn—together—what the community of the church is all about and why being a part of that community is so very important, not only to us, but for the glory of God's Kingdom. Often when you pick up a book, you are hoping to learn something that will improve your life—which is a noble goal. However, this book is different. It is my hope that from this book, you learn not only how to experience abundant life in Christ, but also how you fit in the greater community of faith and therefore, improve the body of Christ as well. We'll never be a vital church without a clear understanding of God's call to live life together—in community.

The culture in which we live is a challenging place to enact this truth. All the advances in technology and communication do simplify our lives, but they also contribute to our isolation. Clearly, this affects us as individuals, but I also think it impacts the church. Thanks to today's new technologies, we don't actually have to go to church anymore, do we? We can just listen to the podcast, or watch the sermon online. We don't ever have to speak to another soul. No doubt, the church as a community is being redefined, and I believe using technology to extend our reach is a positive thing. However, we must work harder than ever to draw individuals deeper into community. Outside of community, we will never become the men and women God created us to be. Don't get me wrong. I love that our church can reach people through Twitter, Facebook, and live streaming webcasts of our worship services. However, we cannot stop there. We were designed to be in community and we cannot experience the fullness of God's grace if we are not living life as part of the body of Christ.

Empowered by God

I know this can seem daunting. It is messy and makes us vulnerable. It can seem impossible, which is why Paul's words are so empowering. We were all baptized into one body, by and with one Spirit—the Spirit of God in Christ. We are the incarnation of Christ in the world, thus true community happens only as He fills us. The more we fall in love with Christ—the more we identify with His plan and purpose for our lives, the more the things of this world will become *less* important. Our unity in Christ unites us in a far more powerful way than any earthly barrier might divide us. In *Love One Another*, Gerald Sittser writes:

> *"The more genuine and the deeper our community becomes, the more everything else between us will recede, the more clearly and purely will Jesus Christ and His work become the one and only thing that is vital between us. We have one another only through Christ, but through Christ we have one another—for all eternity."*

Only because the Spirit of God lives in us, are we—a sinful, selfish people—able to experience the community that God intended for us. Why do you think the church still exists today, despite centuries of mistakes? The Spirit of God is at work. How do you think twelve men with relatively no education, on the outskirts of society, lead a religious movement that overtook the entire planet? The Spirit of God is at work.

Last year, a young woman with a dysfunctional family came to work at our church. She proceeded to discover faith, get baptized, and join a small group in which she experienced grace and love so profound, she found healing in regard to two abortions she had as a young woman. One Sunday she shared her testimony, and a DVD of that service was taken to the county jail and shown to 34 incarcerated women. Afterwards, 17 of those 34 women prayed for healing in their own lives from abortions in their pasts. How does that happen? Simple—the Spirit of God in us.

The Spirit of God who lives and reigns in us—and who draws us together as one body—makes the impossible, possible. The Spirit is the one who empowers us. It does not depend on our strength or the resolve of our will. That is the power of community—it is the power of the Spirit of God at work through a broken, humbled people. My prayer is that God will create a hunger in all of us to connect deeply into a church community somewhere—to not be satisfied by an individualistic expression of faith—but instead, be empowered by the presence of the Spirit as we live out our lives in the context of other believers. What a gift God has given us, and I pray that you will find a community to bear witness of His love to the world around you.

10

"All the believers were one in heart and mind. No one claimed that any of his possessions was his own, but they shared everything they had."

ACTS 4:32

"I'll gladly pay you Tuesday for a hamburger today."

WIMPY, POPEYE THE SAILORMAN

It had not been an easy divorce: legal wrangling, name calling, fighting over dividing up the possessions. Bitter. Ugly. And then there was the matter of who would get the house. It was their dream home, the home they built together and assumed they would live in the rest of their lives. She desperately wanted the house. She had poured over every detail, making it feel like a home. It was peaceful to her—a refuge— at least until the other woman entered the picture. But she didn't get the house. Her soon-to-be ex-husband and his new girlfriend were going to get the house and live her dream. On her last night in her beloved home, she set the dining room—candlelight and soft music—and feasted on a pound of shrimp, caviar and a bottle of Chardonnay. She delighted in the meal, and had anyone been there to witness it, they may have noticed a devilish smile playing across her face. When she finished eating, she methodically hid a few shrimp, dipped in caviar, in the hallows of the curtain rods, in each and every room of the large house. The next morning she said goodbye to the house and drove away for the last time.

The ex-husband and his girlfriend were delighted to move in. He felt a smug sense of self-satisfaction at having won; he and his new wife reveled in discussing their future in their beautiful "new" home. The first few days were bliss, but then they started to notice an odor. Faint at first, the smell grew worse until it was completely overwhelming. They tried everything—deep-cleaning, exterminators, steaming the carpets, checking the air vents—but nothing worked. Finally, they called in a fumigation company. They moved out while gas canisters were set off to kill the odor. They replaced all the carpet. Still, a foul, pungent odor consumed the house. People stopped coming over. They couldn't sleep. The maid quit. Finally, they decided moving was their only option. They had to sell the house. The problem with that, of course, was that after six months on the market, the odor was as strong as ever and no one wanted to buy it. Word got out. Eventually, the realtor stopped showing the house and the couple took out a second mortgage to buy a new house and leave the stench behind, regardless of the financial loss.

Right about that time, the woman called her ex-husband to see how things were going. Despite their hostile past, he shared the complete saga of the rotting house. After some strained small talk, she shared how much she missed the old house and offered a reduced settlement in exchange for the house. He agreed on a price for the house—1/10th of the value—and they signed the papers later that day. He was grateful to unload the wretched home and be done with it. A week later, as a final act of aggression towards his ex-wife, the couple packed up every last fixture she had loved...*including the curtain rods.*

I don't know if this story is true or not, but it certainly could be. It's funny, in a sick sort of way, but mostly, it is a sad picture of our society's selfish and growing obsession with things. We know it's possible. We know people can completely lose their perspective when it comes to their possessions. I suppose it's pretty easy for us to sit back and judge others: "Oh yes, people can be like that," as if it somehow doesn't apply to us. The reality, however, is that it *does* apply to us. We love our things. I know I love my things. We work hard for our things. We do. Left unchecked, however, it is easy to fall into the trap of being consumed by those very things, to the detriment of our spiritual life in Christ. If we fall into the trap of pursuing abundance in our world, we will never experience the abundance of Christ. It's that simple.

Don't get me wrong, I love our system. I love our capitalist democracy. I wouldn't have it any other way. However, we must come to terms with the reality that capitalism is based on consumerism. The growth of our economy depends upon our consumption. How do companies get us to keep consuming?

They foster our discontent. They work very hard to convince us what we have is not enough. They strongly suggest that something new might be the secret to our eternal happiness. When the government was desperate to boost our sagging economy, what did they do? They issued tax rebate checks so that we would spend more money. This is modern-day America, people. I'm not sure why we're surprised. When our thinking drifts away from the all-sufficient power of Christ and toward what the world tells us will make us happy, this is what we get. It is a vicious cycle.

This temptation related to consumerism is nothing new. This phenomenon has affected Christian communities throughout history. Gordon Crosby, the founding pastor of Church of the Savior in Washington, D.C., explains it this way: "Christian communities begin with a strong sense of devotion, which expresses itself in a life of discipline, much like the early church described in the book of the Acts. Communities organized around devotion and disciplines tend to produce abundance. Through their discipline and devotion to others, they gradually accumulate wealth in a variety of forms. They prosper. However, in nearly every instance, that prosperity breaks down and leads to decadence."

It is easy to get distracted. We are in danger of allowing the decadence of our culture to suck us into a vortex of materialism from which we cannot extricate ourselves. And the Christian community is not immune. I believe the Church— the body of Christ—is also in trouble. Has our culture impacted the Church to the extent that we no longer see God's provision and His commands in regards to our giving? Could our unhealthy dependence on material things be what is causing us to miss the vital, abundant life God desires for us?

Learning From the Early Church

Thankfully, we are not the first people to struggle with earthly, human desires. The book of Acts details the life of the early church and their struggles to understand a "new life" in Christ. They had to learn how to cope with their desires for the things of this world. Clearly, this was a group of people who experienced the hope and blessing of God because they were centered on worship and discipleship. However, as this community grew, they learned there was another key ingredient to fully receiving the blessing and power of the Holy

Spirit—generosity. Part of the abundance they experience stemmed from their faithfulness in stewardship.

I cannot discuss what it means to have a vital life in Jesus Christ without clearly stating that such a life is one marked by faithful stewardship and a generous spirit. A vital Christian life is one that gives itself away, not only spiritually, but financially. Now, to be sure, we would rather not talk about money. We get uncomfortable and squirmy in our seats when the subject of money comes up. In our minds, it's no one's business but our own. However, let's think about that. If the Bible discussed money more than any other single subject, why should it not be discussed with great regularity in the church? Should we not be talking about the things that Jesus talked about, including money?

Luke, the author of Acts, was an eyewitness in the days of the early church. He recorded what happened so that churches throughout future generations could learn from their experiences. Specifically, he says in Acts 2:45, "Selling their possessions and goods they gave to anyone as he had need." Clearly, stewardship was at the forefront of their spiritual disciplines and vital to the community's life. Before I go any further, let me put your mind at ease. I am not advocating that you sell all your possessions and give all your money to the poor. That is not my expectation nor is that the point.

The actions of these early believers were not recorded so as to become the end-all, be-all model. God does not command us to "sell all our possessions," although that is what the disciples in the early church did. The disciples in that community assessed their situation and the needs of those around them. From that, they discerned that selling their possessions and giving was what God was calling them to do. We, too, should take the same approach. What are the needs around us, what are God's commands, and what is He calling us to give in regards to our money? There are important lessons to learn from Acts, which apply to the context of our lives today.

If we want to experience an abundant life in Christ, we must radically reshape our attitude toward the things of the world. Consider Acts 4:32: "No one claimed that any of his possessions was his own, but they shared everything." They did not eschew all possessions; the Bible clearly says that the members of the church did have possessions. They worked and earned and bartered and over time they accumulated some things, and in some cases, wealth. The radical difference between the early church and most Christians today was their clear understanding of the source of those possessions, such that they did not "claim them" as their own. They didn't see themselves as the owners of what they had, but rather stewards. God was, and is, the owner of all that we have.

When I was a kid, my Dad had a 1966 red Ford Mustang. He was the original owner and kept it in immaculate condition. By the time I was able to drive, it had already become a classic American automobile. I *loved* that car. From time to time, out of the goodness of his heart, my father allowed me to drive it. I cannot tell you how special it made me feel. I knew that his allowing me to take that car out was a true expression of his trust in me. I was also acutely aware that the car was not mine. I was but a momentary steward. I drove that car with great care to honor my father. I can assure you that I did not do anything to that car, including filling it with gas, unless I consulted him first.

I think this is exactly how we should treat our possessions. James 1:17 reminds us that, "every good and perfect gift is from above." Everything we have belongs to God. It is our privilege to watch over these gifts and use them in a way that honors the owner, our Father. God has entrusted us as stewards of His things. We should understand that sacred trust as an honor and a responsibility. Just like me with my Dad, we need to do a better job of consulting the owner before we get too busy spending what belongs to Him.

Sadly, this is the antithesis of how most of us live today. Our culture extols the virtue and value of personal ownership and individual rights. We want to claim and own everything. Even as believers, we cannot help but think that we own our things, primarily because we are the ones who invested the hours and sacrificed the time and got the job and created the outcomes and earned the money. We are proud to display what we have as a sign of our success or worth among our peers. And it starts early on. For many babies, "mine" is one of the first words they learn.

What's more, we are compelled to amass more things, even when we don't have the means to do so. The age of consumer debt and the proliferation of credit cards have created a shift in our attitudes about spending. We don't have to wait until we have the money for something. We just buy it on credit. Instant gratification. That attitude was the single biggest cause of the economic collapse of late 2008 and early 2009. It's no wonder we're not living abundant lives. We have too much stuff to keep up with, too many things to pay for; we're stressed and we have to keep working in order to juggle it all. We don't have time to dwell on the things of God. Essentially, because of our myriad of financial commitments, we can no longer afford to be generous. How sad.

God says we need to reshape our attitude towards what we have such that it reflects the *true* reality—His reality. *All* that we have comes from God. All that we have is ours on a temporary basis only. This should be so obvious, but we are absolutely missing the point. The hard reality of life is that no matter how long we work or how many possessions we amass, at some point we die, and as they say, you can't take it with you. In the gospel of Matthew, Jesus says, "Store up for yourselves treasures in heaven." Why? Those are the only treasures that last.

Until we understand that everything we own is on loan, that God is the true owner of all things, we will always be enslaved, fooled into believing that our things validate and define us. The vital Christian life is one that looks at possessions and holds them with open hands such that God is able to use us and those gifts according to His plan and purpose.

The Source of Blessings

When this truth penetrates our lives, then our grip on our things loosens. We become more generous, and in fact, can become the source of God's blessings for others. Our faithful generosity and stewardship is what leads to power and blessing in the community of faith and in the lives of those who are in need. I will never forget the overwhelming feeling I had when I sponsored my first child through Compassion International. I had a picture of a little boy and I was so proud that the money I gave was helping to change his life. It was a great lesson to me then, and one that continues to influence my stewardship today.

Right after Luke describes the way people gave in Acts 4:32, his next words are, "With great power, the apostles continued to testify to the resurrection of the Lord and much grace was upon them." As a result of their stewardship and generosity, the apostles—and in essence, the ministry of the church—was empowered to share the word and accomplish what God had called them to do. As a result, grace was showered upon them.

Grace is when God gives us gifts and goodness that we do not deserve. When God's people mature in their understanding of giving, grace is poured out on them and others in powerful ways. I'm not talking about financial prosperity. This is not a get rich quick scheme. However, when we are good stewards, we will begin to experience the blessings of His grace, His peace, His healing touch, His transforming hand, and His life-changing power. You see, we talk about wanting to see God's mighty hand do mighty things, but do we really think God is going to honor and bless us when we are withholding, in disobedience, what actually belongs to him? I don't think so.

In 2 Corinthians 9:6-8, Paul illustrates another important giving principle: the law of sowing and reaping. "Remember this: whoever sows sparingly will also reap sparingly, and whoever sows generously will also reap generously...and God is able to make all grace abound to you, so that in all things at all times, having all that you need, you will abound in every good work." In the agrarian culture of the early church, farmers inherently understood this, but I'm not sure it has the same impact today. Here is the gist: if you don't plant much seed, you won't get a big crop. If you plant a lot of seed, the odds are far better that you will bring in a much larger crop. We know this is how the world works.

If we want to reap an A on our biology test, we must sow seeds of good study. If we want to reap a successful company, we must sow seeds of investment in the lives of our employees. If we want to reap a healthy marriage, we must sow seeds of trust, loyalty and mutuality. It is the law of sowing and reaping. As such, if we learn to be faithful in our giving and consistently generous, God will meet our every need so that we will be able to accomplish every good work that He desires. I don't know about you, but that sounds like a vital life to me. I did it—I took God at His word—and He showed me it was true. I cannot tell you the number of people I have encountered over the years who have learned to be generous in exactly the same way. They have faith that if they give, God will pour out the power and blessings of His grace in abundant ways, and then He does. To be sure, those blessings may not come in the way we think they should, but they do come.

Here's the bad news: Right now, the average person in America gives 2.66 percent of his or her annual income to charitable causes. Some of that may go to a faith community or church, but much of it goes elsewhere. According to data from UNICEF and emptytomb.org, if the Christian church in the United States tithed 10 percent, as God asks, we would raise an additional 86 billion dollars. Do you know how much it would take to fund the worldwide cost for unmet basic human needs like food, clean water, shelter and medical care? Current estimates say 80 billion dollars. We could meet all those needs and still have six billion dollars left over for evangelism. Similarly, when the early church got serious about stewardship, Acts 4:34 says, "There were no needy persons among them." All the needs were met by the generosity of the church. Based on that, it sounds like God knew what He was doing when He asked us to give our tithes and offerings.

So, let me ask you: how do you want to give? What kind of seed do you want to sow as a believer who claims the name of Jesus Christ? Do you want to sow in generosity that leads to the power of God at work? Or shall we sow sparingly, trusting only in ourselves? To put things in perspective, J.I. Packer has said, "As long as the church is alive, it is going to cost time and money. And when she dies, it won't cost us another minute or another penny." If you want to live a vital, healthy, abundant Christian life, then give faithfully.

God Means Business
I once heard someone say that God gave commandments, not suggestions. God is loving and kind, but He is not a pushover. We need to take Him at His word and that includes our stewardship. God is absolutely serious about the discipline of giving. This is the part where you are going to be tempted to put down this book and go read a magazine. This is the real stuff, this is where the rubber-meets-the-road.

I believe we treat this command to give as if it is a negotiation: "Well, God, you didn't really come through on the Baker deal—or in my marriage—or in my health, so I think I'll give two percent this year." Perhaps in our imagination, God counters with five percent and we compromise and give three percent. But this is not a negotiation.

Everything we have comes from God, and He has asked us to give 10 percent of what we have to the church, so that she might fulfill her ministry and calling. In addition, He wants us to give an offering to help provide for the needs of others in our world. He wants us to help support the needy, the aliens, the widows and the orphans. The concept in Scripture is not just tithes, but tithes and offerings.

In Acts, Luke is very clear about this idea. First, in Acts 4:34, he describes how people would, from time to time, sell their land and give the money to the church for distribution. It was that kind of sacrifice that made ministry to the needy in their community possible. He talks about a man named Barnabas who sells some of his land and gives the proceeds to the church. Then, in Acts 5:1, Luke describes a situation where someone was not generous and the consequences that followed. He introduces a man named Ananias who also sold a piece of his property, but instead of giving all the money to the apostles, he kept some back for himself. He gave it to the church as if he were making a complete sacrifice. He gave it trying to create the appearance of faithful giving, but he was lying to God and to the church. Soon after, he and his wife fell over dead. It's gruesome and graphic, but it serves as a stark example of God's view regarding our stewardship. He takes this very seriously. In essence, God is saying, "Here's Barnabas and how he gave. Here's Ananias and Sapphira and how they gave. Now, think about your own stewardship."

Transformed to Give
No doubt, God is serious about this, but we will never understand why giving is important until we have been changed and transformed by the Gospel. It is much like the illustration of the pedestrian and the car that I shared earlier. If you see that a car is about to crush you and someone knocks you out of the way, you respond with gratitude. You want to offer something to that person. However, if you don't see the car, then the person who knocks you out of the way is nothing more than a nuisance. The same is true in our giving. If we realize the magnitude of what God has done for us in Jesus Christ, that He has saved us from certain death, then our hearts are filled with the desire to honor and obey Him. Our hearts want to offer Him all that we have out of gratitude for what He has done. However, if we don't really understand

our need for a savior, then we will never understand why we should part with our precious things. Why should we? For that reason, giving is not a financial decision. It is a spiritual one. It is a matter of heart.

Further, when the Gospel changes our lives, we realize it is the singular hope of the world. As such, the building of God's Kingdom become the priority of our giving. How could it not? If Christ alone is the hope of the world, the only possible answer for the pains we see others enduring, then we are compelled to support that cause. Sure, the American Heart Association is a worthy cause. The United Way does great things in our communities. There are many organizations worthy of our support, but those organizations *are not the singular hope of the world*. Those organizations do not deal in ultimate, eternal things. The priority of my giving, my tithe, is to Christ's Church. Then, I will give an offering to care for people in other ways.

Our Hidden Disobedience

Finally, God has brought me to a challenging realization of late and it is this: the reason that 94 percent of God's people do not tithe is because they have no accountability in regard to their finances. (Yes, according to SpiritResources.com, only 6 percent of American Christians actually tithe.) Think about it. 94 percent of people who profess a deep and active faith in God *do not obey* Him when it comes to their money. The level of disobedience is stunning. People are willing to talk about many challenging issues in their lives. They will discuss and share about their alcoholism, their pornography addiction, their infidelity, their lack of ethics in the workplace, their gambling—you name it. We are willing to openly share many things, but we never talk about money. I have been in countless small groups. I have heard hundreds of testimonies. I have been in several accountability and covenant groups. Never have I heard anyone disclose what they make or how much they give. Our money is the last bastion of our control.

It is almost considered socially improper to discuss money. We'll talk about the "great deal" we got on our house or our car, but we never say how much. We talk about our "ten percent" raise, but we never talk about the total. We talk about our support of various causes, but we never say how much we give. Honestly, in your life, how many times have you heard someone discuss what they make, what they spend, what they give, and what they save? It just does not happen. We have set up a "Christian system" that allows us to keep that information tucked away and hidden, and because it's hidden, *no one can speak into our lives about our disobedience.* We'll reveal everything else, but we will never reveal that, and so we go right on living according to our will —and outside the will and plan of God.

If we ever want to get free in regard to our money, if we ever want to experience the true abundance of life in Christ, we have got to change this system. No question, it will not be an easy change.

I have had a discussion with the director of our small group ministry about how to enact this in our church. Together, we have built training with our group leaders to bring our church towards this awareness. However, even for the most gifted leader, talking about money still feels like being naked in front of a crowd. Nothing makes us feel more exposed then having others know what we make or what we spend. This feeling of nakedness largely stems from our belief that what we have defines us. Our identity is held in what we have, therefore, we spend more than we have to make sure the world is convinced about our worth. If we live with that notion, we don't want others to know what the real foundation is. We don't want to be exposed. However, until we are exposed, we'll never change. We'll never get healthy and free in regard to our money.

Before you get too exercised about this, I am not advocating that you stand up in front of a large group and discuss your income. Instead, I believe we must allow a small group of others to know our financial situation and have permission to speak into us about it. I know I need someone to say to me, "David, are you being faithful with your money?" In the absence of that, answering to no one, I am far more prone to do what I want and to do what I want right now. Thus, in my life, I have two men who know all the grim details. In fact, to illustrate my point, my wife and I led a marriage retreat this year, and in our session on money, we laid out on a whiteboard our entire financial picture. You should have seen the looks on the faces of the people there. Did we feel exposed? You bet we did, but I can also tell you we felt convicted. We felt accountable. I wanted to be sure that I was being obedient. It helped us immensely.

This past month, I taught our new member class on the topic of stewardship. As we often do, we invited one of our elders to give a brief testimony on the impact of faithful stewardship in his life. He prefaced his remarks by sharing that he had read Acts 5 (Ananias and Sapphira) in preparation and realized he had better be sure he was tithing faithfully before he opened his mouth. He did some math, and in his words "needed to write a few checks" before he spoke. Why did he do that? Speaking to a group about his stewardship made him feel accountable to that group and to God. As a result, he became very obedient in his giving. I loved it. After he spoke, I hardly even felt the need to teach. It had all been said very clearly.

Learning the Dance
In closing this chapter, I realize this may be the most sensitive and challenging topic I've addressed in this whole book. This is tough stuff. Giving—generosity—is such a hard concept because it flies in the face of everything our culture would lead us to believe is true. Martin Luther said there are three stages of Christian conversion. First, the heart gets converted and we feel God's love. Next, the mind is converted and we accept intellectually what we've already felt in our hearts is true. Finally, the will is converted and we begin to yield our desires to the truth we know in both our heads and our hearts. We know it. We feel it. Then, we start to yield our will to God's will. A big piece of the conversion of our will is letting go of our desire for more things and accepting our role as stewards of God's things in this world. When we grow toward that, we find amazing freedom in our finances.

The early church grew—it had power in the presence of the Spirit—because it was centered on Christ, had a clear commitment to worship, and because the believers had a mature, radical attitude toward their possessions. They took God at His word and acted in obedience. As a result, ministry flourished. I want that for you. I want that for all of us.

One of the best feelings you can have in this life is the realization that you've became a funnel for God's resources and are making a difference in the lives of others. It will fill you with a sense of joy and purpose unlike anything you've experienced. When we yield our lives to God and allow His resources to flow through us, He pours out blessings untold, blessings that create the abundant life in Christ we so yearn to experience.

There's an old Jewish proverb, quoted by Abraham Heschel, that goes like this: "A musician was playing a very beautiful instrument and the music so enraptured the people that they were driven to dance ecstatically. Then a deaf man, who knew nothing of music passed by, and seeing the enthusiastic dancing of the people, decided they must be insane." There is no doubt, if you start to live as if everything you have belongs to God, people around you will not understand. They may think you are crazy, but it is only because they cannot hear the music of the Gospel.

Our giving should not be based on a command or performing an obligatory duty. Our giving should be based on the self-giving character of our God, who poured Himself out in Jesus Christ, humbled Himself and emptied Himself, for us. When we truly understand the great gift He has bestowed on us—the gift of our forgiveness and redemption—then our hearts will be transformed. Only then will faithful generosity be natural and abundant.

Until that time, those who have not been transformed by His grace and those who have not truly been touched by His love will see the ecstatic dancing and joyous giving of those committed to Christ and call us crazy. In the eyes of the world it *is* crazy and reckless. However, I can assure you that we're not crazy, just obedient. My prayer is that the joy of the Holy Spirit would move us to generosity, regardless of what a faithless world may think. As we grow in this, I believe God will bless us with an abundance of His grace and power such that we will be able to accomplish all He is calling us to do. What joy! Let's dance!

11

"You are the salt of the earth..."

MATTHEW 5:13

"It is hard to exaggerate the degree to which the modern church seems irrelevant to modern man."

ELTON TRUEBLOOD

"Being salt is not nearly so much about having more pastors and missionaries as it is about having many more committed Christian laypeople thinking strategically about and acting on ways to build the Kingdom in such areas as public policy, advertising, media, higher education, entertainment, the arts and sports."

BOB BRINER, *ROARING LAMBS*

I first met Mike Allen when I was in high school in the fall of 1980. He was in his early twenties and working as a financial analyst at one of the big, hot shot firms in Dallas. He was a *great* basketball player, and slightly less important to me at the time, a faithful Christian man. From what I knew of him, he seemed like an all-around great human being. In general, he was funny, honest, and humble. Through some of my teammates, I had heard about a Wednesday night Bible study that Mike led at Highland Park Presbyterian Church, and he seemed cool enough that I wanted to attend.

Having grown-up Roman Catholic, I had never been to a Bible study before and was entirely unsure about what to expect. What would we do? What would we talk about? What if I did not know the answers? Ultimately, my curiosity trumped my fear and I decided to give it a try. However, when I arrived, I was the only one there. It was awful. I didn't want to be there. Mike was gracious and made small talk, but I was panicking. And I'm sure Mike was thinking, "Oh great, I've done all this work and only one kid shows up." If that

was what he was thinking, he certainly hid it well. Mike treated me as if I was the most important student to ever come
through the doors of a church. We sat down that night, just he
and I, and he made God's word come alive.

We talked about what the Gospel of Matthew had to say
about the life of Jesus. He answered my questions as if they
were the most thought-provoking questions he'd ever heard.
He took time to explain things. He didn't hurry. He tried to
help me understand how the Bible actually applied to the life
that I was living. Finally, he asked how he could pray for me,
and then he did. He prayed. Other than my parents, I had
never heard another person pray for me. And as a shy, insecure teenager, it was one of the most powerful moments of
my life up to that point. That was the night when the spiritual
doors of my heart flew open.

From that day on and for the next two and a half years,
I did as much as I could to be in the presence of Mike Allen.
He loved Jesus and he loved me, and I could not get enough
of those two things. I watched and listened to everything he
said about business and how to live with honesty and integrity. I watched and listened as he fell in love with the woman
he would marry, learning from him how to love and cher-
ish a woman, how to pray with her and build intimacy based
on the love of God in Christ; as he and Melissa gave birth
to their first child, I glimpsed the tremendous responsibility
and wonder of fatherhood. At that time in my life, more than
anyone else in the world, I wanted to be like Mike Allen. He is
one of the primary reasons that I am the person and the pastor I am today. I still have a small, paperback New Testament
sitting on my desk that he gave me. He took the time to share
his life with me—to share Christ with me—and as a result, he
had an incredible impact on my life.

Like me, I am sure you have people in your life who have
shaped you, guided you, and inspired you. To be sure, most
of us have similar influences on the negative side—the power
of influence cuts both ways. It makes me wonder, for all the
people whom I come in contact with on a daily basis, am I
a positive influence? Does my life help influence others toward Christ and His Kingdom? Or does my pride cause others to question their faith or doubt the person of Jesus Christ?
These are tough questions, but ones we must honestly wrestle
with in order to live vital Christian lives, overflowing with

the abundance of God's joy. The problem is we live in a busy, busy world. We live in self-focused communities. We are overcommitted and overworked. As a result, it is very easy to lose sight of how our lives may be affecting others.

After serving the Lord for fifteen years as a missionary to Pakistan, Warren Webster said, "If I had my life to live over again, I would live it to change the lives of people, because you have not changed anything until you have changed the lives of people." If our faith calls us not only to love, but to impact and change the world, are we honestly making a difference? More than twenty years ago, the great Methodist missionary and writer, E. Stanley Jones, was asked to name the number one problem in the church. His quick reply was, "Irrelevance."

Other than identifying ourselves in the modern world, what are we doing to make Christ relevant in a society that increasingly casts Him aside? Other than putting a fish on the back of our cars, what are we doing to show that Christian faith provides answers and meaning in today's culture? I believe it is our lack of focus on these essential questions that can cause our lives to feel empty or meaningless. We are living for ourselves—not for Christ—and at the end of the day, that's not enough. Unless we truly commit our lives to something greater, we are never going to be inspired and challenged. We will never be transformed because we will only grow as far as our isolated hearts and minds can take us.

The Call to Fearless Influence
The larger call of our lives, God's call to live for His Kingdom, is addressed in Jesus' Sermon on the Mount in Matthew. The purpose of that sermon was to encourage and comfort the church, which at that time was just a small group of individuals trying, with mixed success, to lead an alternative lifestyle based on Jesus' teachings. In order to do so, they had to live in stark contrast to the lives of most of the Jews around them, and in many cases, very differently than they had been living up to that point. In the Sermon on the Mount, Jesus says that His followers should be different, that our lifestyle should suggest to the rest of the world that we have discovered something powerful, something transformational.

When describing who we, as His followers, should be He uses words like meek, merciful and pure, and then He calls us to be the "salt of the earth." (Matthew 5:13) What He is asking us to consider is our ability to influence, our relevance in the world around us. Notice that Jesus does not say, "You are becoming the salt of the earth," or "You will be the salt of the earth." No. He is quite clear: when you come to Christ, when you fully offer your life to Him, you *are* the salt of the earth. We have no choice in the matter. If you belong to God in Christ, you are the salt of the earth. That is our identity as a Christian in the world. Period. If you do not live into that identity, then how can you be a healthy person? If you isolate yourself and live only for you, then you are missing an enormous part of what God has planned for your life. In the absence of that thing, your life will lack abundance. You will never be the healthy, vital person He created you to be unless you assume your true identity in Him. You are *salt.*

It is a masterful analogy because it had meaning to every single person in Jesus' time and remains relevant today. Rich and poor, young and old, regardless of time or place, we all understand the properties of salt and what it is used for. In Jesus' time, salt was commonly used as a condiment or spice, to add flavor to bland or poor tasting food; additionally, it was used as a preservative. Without salt, some foods would spoil and thus be wasted. For farmers, waste translated to lost income and as such, salt was a crucial element in a successful agrarian life. Furthermore, Jesus reiterated that salt should never lose its saltiness. It should remain pure. From John Stott and Tim Keller, there are three concepts I want to look at as we try to better understand the notion of influence: penetration, preservation and purity.

Penetration

Salt sitting in the salt shaker is no good to anyone. Salt must penetrate food in order to take effect. Personally, I have never been one to sprinkle much salt on my food, but I have noticed that if you just sprinkle salt on the top of food without mixing it in, you wind up with a few salty bites, followed by a bland dinner. The salt must be worked *into* the food and that is exactly the point Jesus is making. Sitting inside the four walls of a church, we are doing no good for the Kingdom of God. If we are going to be influential, if we are going to change the nature and the flavor of our world, we must be *in* it. We must penetrate our world to the core so that change can be brought about by the power of the Holy Spirit.

As believers, we often act as if it is our goal to remain insulated from the outside world for fear that the world may influence us. In so doing, we forget that it isn't about us; we've been called to influence and impact the world around us. If we never leave the confines of our carefully constructed, safe Christian lives, we will never experience the joy of what it is to serve God, to risk and trust, to be used for His greater Kingdom.

I struggle when I see Christians who spend phenomenal amounts of time and energy investing in Bible studies and small groups, sometimes five or six times a week, yet they do nothing to engage in the "real" world. They have no association with anyone who is not already a Christian. They protect themselves from any situation in which they might encounter a non-believer. Make no mistake, I am not condemning Bible study; of course, we need to be studying the Bible. We need to be deepening our lives in Christ, but if that's all we ever do, we are not living the life to which God has called us. When Jesus called the disciples in Mark 3, he said he called them "that they might be with Him and that He might send them out." We are great at "being with Him," but when it comes to being sent out into the world, well, I'm not sure we always want that. The result, of course, is that we only experience half of God's call and half of His promised abundance. Challenge yourself. Think about how you are following the Lord. What are you doing to penetrate the world around you in God's name? And if not, what is holding you back?

Keep in mind, salt penetrates the food from the outside. As followers of Jesus, we are separate from, but involved in, the world. We are related to, but distinct from, the culture in which we live. This is not our home, but we do live here. We live between the now and the not yet. We come from the Kingdom of God—the shaker, if you will. That is where we are most comfortable, but we must get "shaken" out in order to accomplish our purpose. Just as Jesus was a real, authentic and transforming human being who walked this earth, we too, belong to this world. The example He set for us is clear: He penetrated His world. He went to the powerful, the religious and governmental leaders. He rubbed elbows with the Pharisees, the Sadducees, and Pontius Pilate. He spent time with the poor and needy, the hungry and sick. He brought truth and love and healing. In the process, lives were changed.

Jesus engaged the world. He taught on the hillsides. He allowed the people to respond and He shared dialogue, He listened, and He communicated truth. He shared the radical truth about God's forgiveness, and His perfect and transforming love. Jesus' message was relevant and He took it to the people who needed to hear it most; He didn't force them to seek Him out. He was actively engaged in their world. Why should our lives or our call be any different?

It shouldn't. To be salt in our world means we must radically reshape our understanding of what it means to be called. Here's a dose of healthy perspective: our lives are not about us, but rather about something far greater than us—God's call to be part of His Kingdom on earth. We are part of a much larger story—*the* story—*His* story.

I'll never forget when the U.S. Hockey team beat Russia in the 1980 Olympics. I was in high school and an avid sports fan, so I had already seen plenty of triumphant moments in sports. But watching your team win never gets old! Even so, that particular victory was something altogether different. That single game brought people together in a way I had never experienced. I had never felt like an American the way I did that day. I felt connected to these other people; I felt part of this much larger community—the United States of America. It was exhilarating! I felt proud. And that's what I'm talking about. When you accept that you are part of a much larger body, you will find your life infused with far more significance and purpose. As a result, you will be living in a far healthier manner.

Jesus called us to be the salt of the earth. He intends for us to be influencers for God's kingdom. We must stop thinking that the only people called to ministry are full-time pastors or missionaries living abroad. Our lives are to be our ministry. We are to be salt in our homes, at our jobs, in our friendships. God has placed us each in the middle of a unique circle of influence, and it is our responsibility—and our privilege—to make the message of the Gospel relevant. The number one way that we can change our world is to demonstrate Christ's relevance in every area of life. It is what our faith demands. It is our identity. So, going back to my prior point, where are you encountering people who are not part of God's Kingdom?

In our church, I do annual performance reviews with all my direct reports, and they do the same with their direct reports. One of the questions they have to answer each year is this: "Where are you involved in the community to engage non-believers?" I want them to be intentional about engaging more than just the members of our church, but engaging the non-believing, secular world around us. For example, our Minister of Worship is involved in a number of arts organizations in Orlando. She gets creative energy from them, but it also puts her in a position to build relationships and influence others for Christ. In my own life, I have done this through sports and business organizations. I have coached in secular AAU leagues for years, and let me tell you, that is about as secular as it gets! If you want to find some lost people, go hang out at an AAU tournament. It's all about self. I have been a part of the Rotary Club as well. I do it not because I need to learn better business skills, thought that may happen. I do it because I want to meet business people in our community who do not know Christ so that I can build relationships with them.

In his now classic book, *Roaring Lambs*, Bob Briner writes,

> *"Being salt is not nearly so much about having more pastors and missionaries as it is about having many more committed Christian lay people thinking strategically about and acting on ways to build the kingdom in such areas as public policy, advertising, media, higher education, entertainment, the arts, and sports."*

We can sit back and complain about how bad television is getting or we can get involved in the industry and help make positive programming that represents and promotes our faith and values. Christian singers are often lampooned by the Christian community for "going secular" by attempting to make a name for themselves in mainstream music. I believe our response should be exactly the opposite. We need Christians in the music business to flavor the world with the Gospel. We must stop being afraid of the culture. We must fight the temptation to be indifferent. We must heed God's call to make faith relevant in the world in which we live.

Even as I write this, I know there are people who will immediately think, "He is speaking to someone else. I could never do that." While I understand the feeling, I also believe you are dead wrong. Think about the nature of salt for a minute. The individual grains are incredibly small, but they are not intended to be considered individually; their power is in the whole.

In his book, *Seeing What is Sacred*, Ken Gire tells the touching story of a Young Life leader named Scott Manley. While in high school, Gire was led to Christ by his Young Life leader, a leader who had been led to Christ by Scott Manley. Gire went on to lead one of his friends to Christ, a young woman named Judy, who would later become his wife and the mother of his three children. Later in life, when Judy unexpectedly met Scott Manley at a conference, she threw her arms around his neck and said, "You don't know me, but there's something I have wanted to say to you for a long time. You led my husband's Young Life leader to Christ, and he led my husband to Christ, and my husband led me, and we led our children. Scott, *you* are our spiritual heritage. All of us know Jesus because of your ministry—your influence." Together in that moment, they cried.

You and I may never experience such a chance encounter, but if we live in the world with the intention of influencing others for Christ, we will experience many profound moments all our own. It is here—in God's call to be salt—that we discover something profound and meaningful. In Christ, we can change the world. We might not be able to change all of it, but we can make a difference, little by little, one life at a time. You matter, and your acts of service, both large and small, are influencing the people around you.

A Right Way and a Wrong Way

I think it is important to consider not only the call to influence, but the manner in which we go about it. In 1 Peter 3:15, Peter writes:

> "But in your hearts set apart Christ as Lord. Always be prepared to give an answer to everyone who asks you to give the reason for the hope that you have. But do this with gentleness and respect."

Yes, we are called to flavor the world around us, but we don't want to leave a bad aftertaste. Regardless of whom we may encounter or what their beliefs may be, we need to treat each and every individual as worthy of our love and our respect. Instead of brandishing our Bibles as weapons, we must remember to be gentle. If we try to "influence" others with condescending language or by pointing out shortcomings, we lose whatever potential impact we may have had.

Last year, our church hosted a Focus on the Family conference called *Love Won Out*, designed for people dealing with sexual brokenness, particularly those struggling with same-sex attraction. Naturally, once Orlando's gay community got wind of it, they mobilized and on the first day of the conference there was a 100+ person picket line. They were chanting and waving signs, stopping people as they tried to enter. I watched for a few moments as conference attendees ran the gauntlet of picketers to get to our church, and then I made a choice. I would stay outside with the picketers until the very last one went home. I started with the one closest to me and introduced myself as the pastor of the church. I offered them coffee; I brought them doughnuts. Over the course of several hours, I worked my way through the entire group. I asked questions. I listened. They were stunned. They said that they had never been treated graciously by any other church body and in fact, they were used to being greeted with shouts, ridicule and scorn. They told me their stories. One couple told me how their son had been brutally beaten and killed. They shared the ways they had been hurt by people in the church. Here is the point: because I treated them with grace and dignity, I was able to share my understanding of God's love. And because I had established trust and respect—they listened. Seeds were planted. I didn't harvest any that day, but the seeds were planted.

To be sure, there are times when we need to stand up and make our voices heard, but I doubt that many women seeking abortions have ever been drawn to Christ by an angry man with a picket sign. I doubt many people struggling with same-sex attraction have ever walked into a church as the result of someone yelling "faggot" in their faces. Christ met people where they were. He treated, even the lowliest of society, as those who bore the image of God, and that perspective should always be our starting point with others. Yes, we should be prepared to discuss and defend our beliefs, but in our quest to be "salty," gentleness and respect must come first.

Preservative

Next, let's think about salt as a preservative. Prior to refrig-eration, certain foods, primarily meats and poultry and fish, were rubbed down with salt so that they would last up to six months. The salt allowed things that were decaying to be pre-served. So what did God want us to take from this salt anal-ogy? First, I believe it is a statement about the world in which we live. Jesus would never have called us salt, he would never have charged us to go into the world, if the world was not de-caying. You don't have to look very far to see evidence of this fact. We cannot stop the world from decaying entirely, but we can help slow its trajectory. When Christians are in the world, we can be used by God to preserve it, to take something that is in the process of decaying and literally reverse that process.

We infiltrate the dark places that are decaying or dying. We must challenge ourselves to look creatively at our cul-ture and find the places that are coming apart. Once we've identified them, those are the places we go into ministry. That is where we love the unlovable. That is where we engage. Consider this, too: In Jesus' time, people did not use salt to preserve potatoes. Why? They were not going to decay. They didn't need salt. Potatoes remain edible for a long time all on their own. I think what often happens is Christians have a particular affinity for serving in places that are not coming apart, places where we are comfortable. We're rubbing our salt on potatoes. We want to serve, but we prefer to serve in places where there is not going to be any conflict, where there won't be any trouble. We want to go share Christ where things are holding together pretty well.

That's natural. However, that is not fulfilling God's call. He wants us to put ourselves in the middle of situations and places that are falling apart and to help preserve them. We are called to be involved in the lives of our families, to work in the media and television industries, and to partici-pate in local government and national politics; we are called to engage with people addicted to substances, to walk with people through grief, to rub shoulders with people who are depressed or homeless, to be involved wherever Jesus would have been involved. Then, by His presence in us, He can slow, if not reverse, the decay.

Several months ago, I got an email from a friend express-ing his tremendous guilt. He told me how as part of his daily commute he passes over the same highway bridge, and just a few days before, as he drove that route, he noticed a man standing with one leg dangling over the railing. Although he felt like he should go back and help the man, he was late, and wasn't sure what he would say. "I'm sure someone else will help him. He probably is just a workman doing early repair work anyway," he justified to himself. The next day my friend discovered that he was one of literally hundreds of people who had passed this troubled man before he jumped from the bridge to his death. My friend was inconsolable. He could not believe he had ignored the urge to go and help the man. I'm sure all of us have missed opportunities like that, but here's what we need to realize: God has placed us here to act as a preservative. We may not encounter the decaying parts of life in such a graphic or literal way, but every day, we are surrounded by people who are hurting—people who are dying on the inside. We are called to go into places that are coming apart, and by the ministry of the Holy Spirit, to bring life. Challenge yourself to serve in places that really need "salt." It will empower you and give your life perspective; it will make you a more vital, healthy human being.

As a pastor, I have my good days and my bad days. There are days when I feel like God is using me and people are responding, but there are plenty of other days when I feel lost in a cloud of emptiness, surrounded by complaints and an avalanche of human need. On those days, I go to the hospital. I leave the office and I visit members of our congregation who are hospitalized because it gives me a deep sense of contributing to God's Kingdom. No matter how frustrated and hopeless I may feel, visiting people in the hospital always restores my spirit. In that place, I am an instrument in God's hands; God's work in me is palpable, and it transforms my attitude about everything else. If you want to live a vital, healthy, abundant life in Christ—serve. Live out God's call to be salt, a preservative. I promise you will be transformed.

Purity
Finally, salt needs to remain pure. Jesus says, "If the salt loses its saltiness, how can it be made salty again? It is no longer good for anything, except to be thrown out..." In other words, we must keep ourselves salty. We must keep ourselves pure. A chemist will tell you that the properties and principles

of salt cannot be changed. It is impossible for salt *not* to be salt. The only thing that can alter the properties of salt is if it becomes diluted. If salt is mixed with other substances, water in particular, it becomes a white, powdery mess, which Jesus said was only good for trampling under feet. As Christians, we are constantly in danger of being diluted by the influences of the world around us. We must always be on guard and not allow ourselves to be watered down and weakened to such a degree that we lose our ability to influence.

Sadly, that "watering down" seems to be happening in many places. Churches are straying from the centrality of Christ as the sole means of our salvation, watering down the Gospel such that it is only one way to God among many. As our message is weakened, and culturally adapted, we lose our saltiness. We cease to be relevant when our message is indistinguishable from the culture around us. Remember, the Sermon on the Mount was all about our call to be different. In his book, *Introduction to the Beatitudes*, Martin Lloyd-Jones, the wonderful British preacher and author said, "The glory of the gospel is that when the church is absolutely different from the world, she invariably attracts it." That's it! When we allow ourselves to be watered down for fear that we might be offensive or judgmental or exclusive, we lose the very distinctive nature of our call that attracts people. The world is not searching for commonplace answers. They have already tried the culture's answers and found them wanting. They are looking for something different—something transforming. It is that difference—the saltiness—of the church that will ultimately attract and satisfy.

When I was in college, I discovered this truth in living form. I had decided to follow Christ, but I also wanted to be in a fraternity. It wasn't an easy path, and I certainly didn't make all of the right choices, but it became a tremendous opportunity to discover my own saltiness. I did not brandish my Bible as a weapon, but I tried to live among my fraternity brothers with a quiet, but compelling truth. I would attend the parties and have fun, but I did not drink. Many of our interactions centered on intramural sports, and because I was a decent athlete, I was able to earn respect through competition. Even so, I was not always invited to every activity.

Here's what I discovered: because I did not allow their influence to dominate or change me, they slowly began to respect me for my position, and even seek me out for conversation. When they wanted to talk about something real, they came to my room. I had many emotional, vulnerable conversations with these big, tough frat guys, sitting on the sofa in my room. We talked about a mother's cancer, or a family member's death, failing grades or a broken relationship—or whatever hardship they were dealing with. I believe my life became attractive because it looked different. By no means was I perfect, but I was trying to live in a faithful manner. That choice bore fruit. Even in my ministry today, the same pattern holds true. My sons have played basketball for various teams all their lives, and as a result I've crossed paths with many interesting sets of parents, many of whom do not follow Christ. I actively try to build relationships with them, to defy their stereotypes of whom and what a pastor can be. (My son once told me that a member of his team asked him if I just prayed and burned candles all day.) I'm a real person—just like anybody else; the difference is I'm trying to follow Christ. We make small talk during the games, nothing serious—but when the chips are down, the phone rings in my office.

Not long ago, I received one of those phone calls. He was the president of a local bank, and someone had tried to commit suicide in the parking lot of one of his branches. He had never dealt with such a tragedy and he wasn't sure how to cope. He asked a few questions, and I did my best to encourage him, and that was all it took to get him through the ordeal. I certainly didn't do any grand thing, but I was honored and grateful that he called. Another such phone call came from a parent diagnosed with lung cancer, dealing with end of life issues, and asking if I would baptize him. Again, it was a holy moment. Somehow, my life looked different and while they may or may not have understood why, they were looking to me for answers when nothing else seemed to work. It was not because I'm a pastor. It was simply the result of living life as a Christian, out in the world. That's our call. Live courageously. Follow Christ. Don't allow your faith to be diluted by the world, and you will find that others are attracted to you because you stand out, because you are different.

When Jesus Christ walked the earth, His was a ministry of relevance and powerful influence. What he said and did changed people. In his book, *The Incomparable Christ*, Kenneth LaTourette says:

"No life ever lived has been so influential...as that of Christ. Through it, millions of people have had their inner conflicts resolved. Through it, hundreds of millions have been lifted from illiteracy and ignorance and have been placed upon the road to growing intellectual freedom and control over the physical environment. It has done more to allay the physical ills of disease and famine than any other impulse, and it has emancipated millions from chattel slavery and millions of others from thralldom to vice. It has protected tens of millions from exploitation by their fellows, and it has been the most fruitful source of movements to lessen the horrors of war and to put the relations of men and nations on the basis of justice and peace."

You are called to be salt. Your life matters. It is up to you to determine how you will wield the most influence. It may mean having a Christian bumper sticker on your car, or maybe not. Perhaps you will have the most influence by quietly infiltrating the world around you with confidence and conviction. God has empowered you to be the salt of the earth. You are a child of the living God, and your life is a part of His master plan for the Kingdom at large. Live into that. Spend time with God each day. Enrich your life in the presence of other believers. Then, go out and influence your world. Such commitment is one of the most rewarding parts of living a vital, abundant life as a disciple of Jesus Christ.

Part Three

STAYING HEALTHY

12

"We have come to share in Christ if we hold firmly till the end the confidence we had at first."

HEBREWS 3:14

"To me, consensus seems to be the process of abandoning all beliefs, principles, values and policies in search of something in which no one believes... What great cause would have been fought for and won under the banner, 'I stand for consensus?'"

MARGARET THATCHER, 1981

Basketball is in my blood. Always has been, always will be. My earliest memories are of hours spent in my driveway, shooting ball after ball at the basket affixed to the top of our garage. My Dad would join me when he got home from work, and I would shoot until I couldn't see anymore. Throughout my elementary years, as I played on various school and YMCA teams, my dad was often my coach. At times, we had practice in that same driveway: eight little boys crammed onto a thirty square foot pad of concrete. Those are sweet memories.

Once I graduated to junior high, things changed a bit. I attended Dan D. Rogers Junior High and played for a man named Bill Robbins. Coach Robbins was an interesting man—a large man, with an even larger personality—who thrived on what I would call "coaching intensity." He yelled and screamed a lot and made it very clear that we were to be tough. Toughness was king. It didn't matter that we were eleven, we were expected to play like men. Fatigue or fear or even thirst were considered signs of weakness. If Coach Robbins sensed you were tired—or if you were dumb enough to *admit* that you were tired—he would take you out of the game and that was it. What's more, you heard it about it for days afterward. "Swanson couldn't even make it through the first quarter." That attitude influenced my playing days from that time forward.

When I transferred to a new junior high and even into high school, I believed that I could never show fatigue. If I was in a game, no matter how exhausted I was, I never allowed it to show for fear I would get taken out of the game. That all changed when I began playing for my high school varsity coach, and one of my life mentors, Bo Snowden. Coach Snowden went home to be with the Lord only recently, but he remains one of the three most influential men in my life. He was an intense, tough coach, but he also lived a life of faith and integrity that permeated everything he did. When he was critical, you always knew his words were intended to make you better. Outside of my family, he was the first person who ever truly believed in me, and I'll always remember him for that.

When practice began in the fall, he drilled us on the fundamentals, but also, he taught us his philosophy of coaching. He said that we were going to be a well-conditioned team, so we were running wind sprints all the time. Even so, he also told us we needed to be aware of when we were tired. He believed that when we were tired, it would negatively affect our performance, and thus the entire team. Naturally, that got my attention. He told us what happens when the body gets too tired: your legs stop providing the lift for your shot, and your shooting drops off; your thinking even gets fuzzy, your decisions aren't as sharp and your defense suffers. "When you're in a game, give it all you've got, and when you get tired, hold up your hand, and I'll send in a sub." The substitute would always bring out a towel to the player he was replacing, and he would not let go of that towel until he had all the information on who he was supposed to guard and what defense we were in.

When we came out, he promised he would try to get us back in as soon as he could. I reluctantly took him at his word. And sure enough, when I was tired, I'd hold up a hand, and I'd come out. When I did, my other teammates on the bench would encourage me, the manager would bring me a drink, the assistant coach would go over some pointers on how the game was unfolding and after a couple minutes, I'd get back in the game, much more capable of playing well than had I not rested.

I don't know about you, but I have often thought that we need this same approach in life. We need a "tired signal." We need a signal to let the Lord know we need a couple minutes on the bench. Life can be exhausting, demanding, overwhelming. And when we start to feel that way, we don't think clearly, our decision-making gets fuzzy, our defense mechanisms are slow and we find ourselves susceptible to temptation. In those moments, wouldn't it be great if we could just turn to God and hold up the "tired" signal—just raise a hand—so He could momentarily take us out of the game? I can picture it now. The Holy Spirit would bring me a drink while my fellow believers shouted life affirming words. Jesus would come alongside me and take a few moments to teach me about how to do better in the next phase of life, and then, when I felt ready, I could get on with my life. I would love that.

In my ministry, I hear it all the time. People are worn out. When I ask people how they are, the answer I get the most is, "I'm tired." We don't get enough sleep. When we try to sleep, it isn't restful. We over-schedule our lives. We have no margins. We're afraid to say no. I am reminded of Elijah's moment under the juniper tree in 1 Kings 19, when the angel woke him and said, "Get up and eat, for the journey *is* too much for you." Elijah was flat-out exhausted. He was so tired that he asked the Lord to take him out. The angel's words are true. The journey is too much for us. For that reason, we need the sustenance of the Lord and the support of His body.

My bet is that many of you reading this book are in that place. You're beat, and you're not sure how much longer you can keep going in this game. Naturally that begs the question, if we are constantly worn out, is it possible to experience the abundant life promised in Jesus Christ? No question, when you're tired, such a life can seem a long, long way away.

Staying Strong
It is a question that brings us to a marvelous text in the book of Hebrews. Unlike most books of the Bible, the author of Hebrews is unknown. However, we do know that the intended audience was the Jewish Christians of the early church, a group of believers who had risked a tremendous amount in making their commitment to the Lord Jesus Christ. In those days, if you were a Jewish Christian, you had already made a decision which separated you from most—if not all—of your

family and friends, threatened your economic prosperity and opened you up to a host of negative consequences, including persecution. As you can imagine, the emotional upheaval and loss experienced by these Jewish Christians made them weary—exhausted—and sometimes they simply gave up on their faith. In their fatigue, their defenses grew weaker, and before long, they had turned to the world for comfort and satisfaction. Once healthy and vital, they faltered; they didn't remain strong.

Have you ever witnessed this in the Christian community today? Have you ever seen Christians choose to walk away from the faith when life got complicated? Have you ever watched committed, faithful Christians turn their back on the church and live completely contrary lives? Of course you have—we all have—because life is hard and we are weak. I was stunned last year to learn that a respected church leader in another city had left his wife to run off with another woman, a woman from his congregation. When I asked him how he could make such a choice, he said, "I don't expect you to understand. It's just what I wanted. I just got tired of being good." This faithful man grew so weary living the Christian life that he abandoned it—and his family—altogether. How does this happen? At the very least, I want to understand it better so I can prevent it from happening in my own life down the road.

In our quest to cultivate a vital life in Jesus Christ, one that flows with his promised abundance, we must consider how to maintain our commitment to all the concepts of the preceding chapters. What is it that is going to keep us strong? Even if you believe everything I've said in this book and feel energized about living your life with Christ, the reality is that there are many other pressures being exerted on your life. I think it is safe to say, you are tired. I know I am. How do you and I stay true to what we believe? How do we find vitality in Christ and then—how do we maintain it?

Life is Difficult

First of all, a vital Christian life must begin with an understanding that living as a fully devoted follower of Jesus Christ is *hard*. Living the Christian life is not a piece of cake. It is not something that just happens. Jim Collins wrote a marvelous business book called *Good to Great*, in which he discusses foundational principles for good leadership, including the importance of "ruthlessly confronting your current realities." We won't get anywhere if we can't be honest—with others and with ourselves—about our current situation. As Christians, the first step is admitting that living as a Christian in our world is tough.

I'll never forget the first line of Scott Peck's book, *The Road Less Traveled*: "Life is difficult." It was one of the first books I ever read after becoming a Christian, and it struck me so much that I thought, "OK, I'm going to read the rest of what this guy has to say because he obviously gets it." His honesty made me think he understood the world in which I lived. It's still true—life is difficult. Hebrews 3:12 says, "See to it that no one…turns away from the living God." The author of Hebrews understood that the Jewish Christians were facing challenges, he knew they were tired; he knew they would be tempted to give up and walk away, and he wanted to encourage them and prevent that from happening.

Far too many preachers proclaim a Gospel that says if you love God and worship Him and live your life the "right" way, then God will bless you and your life will be problem-free. They falsely portray a Gospel that says everything you want is just around the corner. Well, the life I live doesn't work that way. I don't know about you, but my prayers are not always answered the way I'd like or on my ideal timeline. God says "no" sometimes, and if you believe that the Christian life means getting what you want from God, you will be sorely disappointed. Because of that same false Gospel, on some level, we believe that God loves us when our lives are going well, and if they're not, well, then God must be unhappy with us. This couldn't be further from the truth.

Your circumstances do not dictate your standing before God. Scripture spells it out—there will be hard times. Do you think God loved Paul? Did he love Peter and John? Did they have lives of circumstantial ease and blessing? No. They lived some of the most faithful, committed Christian lives we have ever seen, and yet they were not financially prosperous and their prayers were not always answered. Following Christ is rich with the abundance of His grace and love, the wonder of forgiveness and the hope of eternity. And yet, we are promised that it won't be perfect or easy. It may well be the hardest life we could have chosen. For us to stay strong, we must ruthlessly confront this reality. We have to know that God loves us and is present with us even when life is hard. Hardship does not mean that His love has faltered or His care has dried up. It just means that we live in a sinful, fallen world and sometimes we bump into it. Scripture reinforces this over and over again:

- Hebrews 10:36: "You have need of endurance."
- Matthew 24:13: "The one who endures to the end will be saved."
- Hebrews 3:14: "We share in Christ if we hold...firm to the end."
- Philippians 4:1: "Stand firm..."
- 2 Thessalonians 2:15: "Stand firm..."
- Ephesians 6:13: "Take up the whole armor that you may stand firm."
- 2 Timothy 3:14: "Hold fast without wavering."
- Matthew 7:14: "The gate is narrow and the way is hard."
- 1 Corinthians 16:9: "There are many adversaries..."
- Jesus said it himself in John 16:33: "In this world, you will have trouble..."

Endure. Persevere. Stand firm. Hold fast. Watch out. These aren't words that are used for people living a lark; these are words of encouragement reserved for those living in the midst of challenges. They are words for those who have been knocked down, and need to find the resolve and strength to get back up. The way of Christ is hard, but it is the only way that leads to true life.

It Can Happen to You
The Christian life is hard, thus there is always a chance of growing too tired, giving up and turning our backs on Christ. We must recognize that we are not immune. Again, Hebrews 3:12 and 14 caution us, "See to it, brothers, that none of you has a sinful, unbelieving heart that turns away from the living God..... so that none of you may be hardened

by sin's deceitfulness." This does not mean you can lose your salvation, for we know that nothing can separate us from the love of God once it is planted in our hearts. However, we are susceptible to turning away. The word for "turn away" is translated literally "to fall away" or some translations use the word "drift." Be careful that as you are living your life, you don't let sin enter into your heart such that you turn away from God, sliding from righteousness into darkness. Part of staying strong is being wise enough to understand none of us are above temptation. There are countless examples of devastation and ruin in Christian communities all over the world.

The insidious thing about this is it can happen little by little, so gradually that you don't recognize it until it's too late. C.S. Lewis said, "The safest road to hell is the gradual one—the gentle slope, soft underfoot, without sudden turnings, without milestones, without signposts." Let's look at a concrete example, one that has been far too prevalent in churches I have served over the past twenty years: adultery.

How do you think most extra-marital affairs start? People do not wake up in the morning, and think, "Today is the day I'll have an affair." It starts slowly. A hundred small decisions over time lead to compromised circumstances, weakened resolve, emotional attachment. Perhaps a marriage is broken, or financial stresses get to be too much. Regardless, all it takes is a little attention from the opposite sex. The attention feels good. It is a distraction from "real" life. Instead of shutting the door to this attention, it is received and over time, full-blown rationalization takes over. Soon sin has deceived both parties and hearts are hardened to such a degree that the behavior no longer seems wrong. And it's not just adultery. This slippery-slope of eroding behavior and beliefs applies to many situations we face on a daily basis. One more drink won't hurt. It's not really a lie. Taxes are too outrageous anyway. It's not cheating; it's just a strip club. We know on some level its wrong, but we rationalize that it isn't *that* bad, it isn't as bad as what other people are doing. We think, "In the grand scheme, this makes me happy, plus I'm not hurting anyone."

I have a good friend in Ft. Myers who loves to deep sea fish. He has a 35-foot boat and one of his favorite things to do is take his buddies out for the weekend to fish. They head out into the middle of the Gulf of Mexico where some of the best deep sea fishing can be found. They'll leave at dusk, have dinner on the boat, then put the boat on auto pilot and go to sleep. By the time they wake up at 5 a.m., they have arrived at their destination, ready to fish. It is a perfect plan, unless you set your compass wrong. Even as little as one degree in the wrong direction can leave you off course by 250 nautical miles in a matter of hours. Can you imagine waking up in that situation? The same is true of our lives. You may think that veering a little off track won't make a difference, but Hebrews reminds us that, in fact, the slightest compromise in our behavior has the potential to change the heading of our entire lives. You don't want to wake up five years from now, hundreds of miles off course, and wonder how you got there. You'll know how. You rationalized sinful behaviors because doing so was easier.

Rest assured, this *can* happen to you! Don't get smug and comfortable in your own righteousness. Don't lie to yourself, reading this chapter and assuming, "Well, that would never happen to me." It *can* happen to you—or me. If you consider yourself immune, you are absolutely ripe to be picked off by the enemy. For that reason, I am constantly putting structure in my life to prevent even the beginnings of temptation. That's why I don't counsel women without my assistant sitting right outside my door. Several years ago, I had a woman come in for counseling whose aggressive demeanor and approach made me very uncomfortable. For this reason I stayed behind my desk. During our visit, she patted the sofa next to her, and said, "Why don't you sit over here. That desk is such a barrier between us." To which I responded, "Yes it is, and that is why I'm staying behind it." I *know* it can happen to me and therefore, I am intentional about guarding my heart and my life.

The Power of Community
I just re-read what I've written in this chapter. Pretty sobering, isn't it? If I closed the chapter at this point, I imagine we'd all walk away feeling discouraged and somewhat hopeless. Life is exhausting and hard; we will be distracted and deceived by our sin; we will be tempted to turn away from God. It's not a very pretty picture, but that isn't the end of the story. God does not leave us there.

Recognizing our weakness, God provides the answer. Hebrews 4:13 says, "Don't turn away...but encourage one another daily, as long as it is called today, so that none of you may be hardened by sin's deceitfulness." Community is the key to our survival. Community is the key to our perseverance and focus on the Lordship of Jesus Christ. In our weakness, we have the body of Christ to give us strength. A vital, abundant Christian life is one that finds itself immersed in community, surrounded by brothers and sisters who care, encourage, support and are willing to hold one another accountable.

The cold, hard truth is that we can't trust ourselves; we need people in our lives to encourage us and hold us accountable to the truth of Christ. We need people who tell us about our blind spots. The encouragement and accountability of the body of Christ is the antidote to the alluring deceitfulness of sin. That said, this is *not* encouragement as you and I tend to think of it. The Greek word used for "encourage" is the word "parakleite" which literally translates "to urge, to strongly plead, to exhort, to beg." It is a word typically used in a military context as the commander of an army attempting to speak strength into his troops before battle. This type of encouragement goes far deeper than sitting around saying, "Hey, Joe, way to go. You're awesome!" This is an image of brothers and sisters, locked in a battle for life, urging one another on, pleading with one another, exhorting each other to keep the faith, to know the truth, to follow Christ. This is one soldier, bombs bursting in the background, urging another not to give up the fight. It connotes the seriousness of what is taking place. This is not fun and games. This is life and death. The stakes are tremendously high.

Every year in Ft. Myers there is a two-week celebration called the Edison Festival of Light which celebrates its most famous resident, Thomas Edison. It culminates with a huge parade downtown. People start staking out their viewing spots on the parade route two and three weeks in advance. It's quite a sight to see miles and miles of sidewalk along the parade route marked with duct tape, spelling out names and marking territory! By the time the event starts, there are thousands and thousands of people lining the three-mile route. Just before the parade begins, there is a 5K race which follows the parade route, and I was blessed to run in that race four years in a row. It was one of the most awesome experiences I have ever had because for all three miles there is a crowd, five and six people deep on each side, and they are all cheering. It felt like running in the Olympics! People you don't even know are shouting encouragement, handing you water, clapping, waving, urging you forward. Every once in a while I would see someone I knew in the crowd, and they would call my name. It would give me chills. I always ran my best times in that race because I felt I was being carried along by the crowd. I could feel the adrenaline rushing though my body. This is the image of Hebrews. This is what the author is talking about.

As we try to run the race of life, it is the community of faith that lines our way and marks out our path. In those moments when we feel we are beginning to tire, when we could be easily tempted to stop or run off course, it is the Church of Jesus Christ who is there, urging, pleading, and encouraging us to keep running the race for Christ.

Church As Institution

I know some people recoil at the sound of the word "church." We hear "church" and we think "institutional" and "formal" and "narrow." We think of churches that are dying and pastors that have failed and abuses that have taken place. Some have said to me, "I want to be with other believers, but I don't want to be in a church." Unquestionably, many churches have failed of late, but let me remind you that churches are inherently flawed. They are made of up of sinful people like you and me, right? How could they be anything other than imperfect?

Even so, God has tasked the church to spread the Gospel around the world, and in order for that to happen, there must be some structure and administration. The sheer scope of the endeavor means some degree of institutionalism. It is the only way to get so many different people moving in the same direction. And God has asked the church to be the incarnation of Jesus to the world. God has asked the church to be His earthly community, and that church, as she has been created, is utterly holy and beautiful. Paul writes of God's love for His Church in Ephesians 5:27, saying "…just as Christ loved the Church and gave himself up for her to make her holy, cleansing her by the washing with water through the Word, and to present her to himself, as a radiant church, without stain or wrinkle or any other blemish, but holy and blameless."

To each one of us called as disciples of Jesus Christ, whether we like it or not, we have been engrafted into His bride, the Church. Thus, it is our call to serve her in such a way that we present her to God even as Christ did, holy and blameless. Yes, the churches we serve and attend may be flawed, but at their core, they are the bride of Christ, and the gates of hell shall never prevail against her. She is not an institution. She is not a bureaucracy. She is not a machine. She is His bride, and thus we are to tend her and love her and nurture her that she might be that body that He yearns for her to be. Our task is not to put down the bride, but to root ourselves within her, building one another up as we experience the blessing of community. It is the key to staying strong and healthy in this life.

Are We Willing?
That leaves us with one final question: are we willing to do this for each other—and are we willing to submit to it ourselves? Being the body of Christ for one another means that we are willing to call people back when they have left the path. It means we must be willing to enact discipline and follow through on how a person becomes restored. It's the hard part of loving someone in the manner of Christ. I believe this element of the Christian life has gotten lost somewhere between our desire to be inclusive and our attempt to not offend anyone. We're so afraid that we might appear judgmental that we have lost the courage and boldness necessary to truly hold one another accountable in Christ. Not to mention, it takes a lot of energy to care for others that much and we've already established that we're tired and overcommitted. Yes, Jesus was gracious and loving, but let's not forget: He was also a righteous Savior. In John 17:3, Jesus said, "If your brother sins, rebuke him. If he repents, forgive him." Jesus knew that part of loving one another means confronting someone when their behavior is compromising the direction of their life, or worse, has the potential to wound the body of Christ as a whole.

Love demands that we not pretend. For example, if you came upon me standing by a busy six-lane road, watching my children darting in and out of traffic, and I said, "Look at them! They're having so much fun." What would you say? Would you think I was a great parent? No! You'd think I was nuts because I was allowing my children to be in danger without doing anything about it. It seems our culture is more about tolerance today—about consensus—than it is about truth. Sin can deceive us into living in dangerous places, and we must have the courage to confront our brothers and sisters in Christ and say, "Come back. You're in a dangerous place. I don't care if you have a bunch of people agreeing with you or not. I love you too much to leave you there." The opposite of love is not hate, its apathy. In community, the key to staying strong in the Christian life is whether or not we love each other enough to say the hard things. It is our obligation as disciples of Jesus Christ and members of His Church to urge and plead with one another daily so that we do not fall away.

Before we get self-righteous in our call to do that, let's remember the flipside is equally important. Are we willing to submit when someone comes to us with rebuke? We have the choice to swell with defensive pride or open ourselves to the tough love of our community. Which is it going to be? During a challenging time early in my ministry, one of my mentors, Dr. Peter B. Barnes, said to me, "David, people are going to be shooting arrows at you all your life. The key to getting through it is learning to spiritually discern which ones need to stick and which ones need to fall off and be forgotten." People are going to say tough things to us, things that may feel like arrows. However, our spiritual hearts must be pliable and humble enough to honestly discern when someone is speaking truth. It they need to stick, they need to stick. Without such words, we never see our blind spots.

When I started as a Senior Pastor in Ft. Myers, Florida, I was young, naïve and a bit idealistic. I had this vision of what the church needed to be, and I was going to get the congregation there in the first three weeks. I came in charging hard, changing things right and left, and before too long, it caught up to me. People were unhappy, and they had a right to be. One particularly irritated woman stopped me in the hallway after a Wednesday night class, poked me in the chest, and said, "You don't love us." Ouch. That hurt. I did love them, but I was changing things so fast that I was not taking the time to be with them. How would they know I loved them? I was moving too fast. Yes, those words felt like an arrow, but I was grateful she told me. I needed to hear it, and my ministry changed significantly after that.

If we want to survive the Christian life and stay true to what we believe, there really is no choice; we must be connected to a strong Christian community. If you are not connected to Christian community, take the necessary steps to engage. Talk to people you trust. Find a church. Yes, that may mean looking around and finding a community that fits you and your family, but don't make perfection the litmus test! Find one that works, then sink your lives deeply into that body and find ways to begin building accountability into your life. It's one thing to be healthy. It's another thing to *stay* healthy. My prayer is that your life would become strong and stay strong as you experience the beauty of the life-sustaining Christian community—the Church.

13

"Do your best to come to me quickly, for Demas, because he loved this world, has deserted me..."

2 TIMOTHY 4:9

"Disregard the study of God, and you sentence yourself to stumble and blunder through life blindfolded, as it were, with no sense of direction and no understanding of what surrounds you. This way you can waste your life and lose your soul."

J.I. PACKER, *KNOWING GOD*

I shared previously that when I was in college, I was in a fraternity. It was not the most glamorous of groups—nor the most organized—but it was a great way to meet people, develop a social life and participate in athletics. For me, those were the positives; getting accepted into the organization, on the other hand, was not. First, you had to be invited to join as a pledge. If you were accepted, you had to endure a probationary period lasting about four months during which you had to "prove your worth," on several different levels. In case you were wondering, yes, it involved hazing, and no, most of it was not very fun.

Even so, there were a few highlights. My particular favorite was a tradition called "going on a drive." This was a ritual that involved the pledge class kidnapping an active member, typically out of his bed in the middle of the night. Once apprehended, the victim would be blindfolded and driven around until the wee hours of the morning, only to be ultimately dropped off in the middle of nowhere with nothing more than his boxers and a quarter. (Yes, I lived before the advent of cell phones. Dinosaurs roamed the earth and a quarter was necessary to make a phone call.) In any event, I survived being a pledge and enjoyed the brotherhood of fraternity life. However, my junior year, the new pledge class chose me. I was sound asleep at 3 a.m. when the pledges burst into my

room, doused me with a mixture of Karo syrup and fish emul-
sion, covered me in a blanket and took me on a drive. When
they finally removed the blindfold and shoved me from the
car, it took me awhile to get my bearings, primarily because
I deduced that I had never been in that part of Dallas. All I
remember is that trash littered the streets and dogs barked
in the distance. Clutching that quarter, it was amazing how
my priorities became crystal clear. Suddenly, I was not thinking about an upcoming test, or the balance in my checkbook,
or even whether or not a particular female was interested in
me. In that moment, nothing mattered. The only thing I cared
about was getting out of that particular situation. And yes, by
the grace and mercy of God, I made it back to my fraternity
house in one piece.

I would imagine you have had a similar moment in your
life, a moment when all the things you thought were important fell away. Perhaps someone you loved was diagnosed
with cancer or you lost your job or you suffered a betrayal
you never thought possible. In those moments, worldly things
don't matter; in those moments, it is all about an eternal perspective. The problem is that most of us don't maintain that
perspective for very long. We may realize what our priorities
should be, but we quickly lose sight of the big picture and
return to selfish living. The attacks of September 11, 2001 are
a perfect example. In the wake of 9/11, as people wrestled
with tragedy and fear, church attendance exploded across the
country. However, within a matter of months, attendance returned to pre-9/11 levels. For a fleeting moment, we all decided to reorder our priorities and get back to the basics of
faith in God, but those moments were short lived. Once the
smoke cleared, we went right back to living according to our
own priorites.

Ask yourself: what is truly important to you in this life? If
you're not sure, I would suggest you check your calendar and
your bank account. Where you spend your time and how you
spend your money will tell you everything you need to know
about your priorities. Are you spending your gifts, resources
and time on the things that you believe are *truly* important?
Would those priorities change in a crisis?

It is easy to talk about our faith and the importance of
our relationship with God, but do we live as if it is a priority?
Are our expressions of faith anything more than lip service?

How much does our commitment ebb and flow? These are questions I ask myself nearly every day. They are questions I ask because I have seen so many people, trying to live vital, abundant Christian lives, who suddenly choose the priorities of the world and walk away. I have seen faithful brothers commit adultery and say to me in the aftermath, "I'm sorry. This is just what I want." I've seen a church leader, a man with a stalwart reputation, lose his job because of questionable money management, all because he was not satisfied with the lavish life he had been living for years. He needed more. And I've seen it happen to pastors and ministers, men and women who have been deeply committed to the Lord and passionate about ministry. At one time, they were strong and healthy, but ultimately, they washed out. They quit. They left and went into business, no longer willing to even talk about their faith. It is scary to watch. I hope it scares you. I ask God to keep me from such an end. I pray that God will keep me strong. I pray that I will put the necessary disciplines into place in order to live a healthy, *enduring* Christian life.

A Case Study

Let's look at an example from Scripture that I think can really help us in this discussion. It is the story of a man once passionate and committed to the Lord who walked away from his faith because he loved the world too much. We need to learn what we can from his life in order to help us avoid the same fate. The man's name was Demas and we actually know very little about him. However, what we do know is a tremendously powerful anecdote which calls us to a deeper commitment to the Lord and to our faith.

Demas is only mentioned three times in Scripture; first, in verse 24 of Philemon, when he is described as a "fellow worker" alongside Paul and several others. We hear of him again in Paul's letter to the Colossians 4:14: "Our dear friend, Luke, the doctor, and Demas send greetings." Finally, in Paul's second letter to Timothy, Paul mentions Demas when he says, "Do your best to come to me quickly, for Demas, because he loved this world, has deserted me..." That just kills me. It's tragic. I just imagine the people of the early church—people like Luke, Paul, Epaphras and Mark—sitting around and asking, "Whatever happened to our old friend Demas? He was so on fire, so committed to the Lord. I just can't figure it out.

What happened?" In a fairly short period of time, perhaps five to seven years, Demas went from working alongside Paul to "utterly deserting" him. And if it happened to Demas, could it happen to you or me? Absolutely.

How does such a downward spiral take place? I believe the answer is found in Paul's description of Demas. He calls him a "fellow worker," meaning Demas was involved in spreading the Gospel of Jesus Christ. Like Paul, Demas was working with Paul in building the Kingdom of God. Further, Paul's description is evidence that he considered Demas an equal, someone who was every bit as committed to following Christ and serving Him in the world as Paul was. Demas was a fellow worker, a comrade, a brother in the fight. Therefore, knowing what we know about Paul, a man who said, "to live is Christ and to die is gain," a man who said, "I count every-thing else in life as rubbish except for the surpassing great-ness of knowing Christ Jesus my Lord," then Demas must have been a man possessed of deep faith and abiding love for Christ as his Lord. We can assume Demas was a man whose mission was one and the same with Paul; he knew who he was in Christ and understood his purpose in serving God. The purpose and priority of his life would have been clear: Christ and Christ alone.

But something changed in Demas' life that caused him to lose his focus and become distracted from that purpose and priority. I think what changed was the cost of his com-mitment, the sacrifice necessary to follow God's call. You see, initially, to be a fellow worker with Paul would have been an exciting, challenging life—an exhilarating experience. They were traveling all over the world and people were re-sponding to their message. Lives were being transformed. People were being healed. It was heady stuff. However, as time wore on, Paul's ministry faced increasing opposition. The more Paul preached, the more persecution and hardship he and his followers endured, until finally it became clear that Paul would die a martyr's death. Association with Paul became a dangerous proposition, one that must have left De-mas asking, "Is my faith—my mission in life—requiring too much of me?"

Furthermore, the text in 2 Timothy 4 says that Demas loved the "present age." As Demas was wrestling with the demands of being a follower of Christ, the lure of the world grew stronger. In the culture of that day, rest assured there were many things to love. New, exciting things were happening. Cities were developing. The influence of Greek life and culture was everywhere, creating not only more wealth, but a host of new ways to enjoy that wealth. Travel was more accessible than ever before. I can only imagine, as Demas looked at the world's attractions and temptations, as he compared the cost of his faith verses the excitement of the world, the world won.

While this is not explicitly spelled out in the text, as Demas considered his life, I believe he realized the world didn't require anything of him. It was easier. Being part of the world demanded no obedience, no commitment, and no sacrifice. It required only indulgence. I believe the weight of that reality was the root of Demas' decision to desert his ministry. Interestingly enough, it doesn't say that Demas was apostate, either. He didn't renounce the faith or say he no longer believed. He did not make a big announcement and share why he thought the resurrection of Jesus was no longer tenable. He simply decided he was not going to commit his entire life to his faith. He reached a point where, in his heart, he loved the world—the present age—more than he loved God.

Can it Happen to me?

I wonder if any of what Demas experienced, any of the choices that he faced, resonate with you? Because they sure do with me. At some point in our lives, we have had that faith moment, a moment when the gracious love of God in Christ penetrates our hearts and we realize the depth of God's love for us; a moment when we come face to face with our own sin and we welcome the cleansing blood of Christ to redeem us from the pit. In that moment, all things become clear. The priorities of life effortlessly line up. Our mission in life becomes simple: to live in obedience to the One who has redeemed us. In that moment, we joyfully give our life to Him in response to the grace that God has lavished on us in Christ. We are, in those moments, like Demas at the outset. We are the enthusiastic, energetic, committed "fellow workers" of Paul. We are striving to serve God and to make His name known wherever we can. Our mission—our priorities—the things we value in life are clear.

Then something happens. Something changes. The high of the moment wears off a bit. We find that our faith requires more of us than we initially thought. We realize that the Christian life can be hard. We begin to feel that our belief in Jesus Christ, while eternally comforting, is too restrictive with its laws and commands and calls for obedience. Sure, we're comfortable with living the church life, attending worship here and there, serving on an occasional committee or ministry team, but standing up for Christ outside of the church, being His representative in the workplace, changing old behaviors and vocabularies and relationships—it is all just too much. We didn't really bargain for the whole package. It feels as if that is taking this whole "faith" thing too far. We are willing to take our faith to a certain point, but we are very careful to never cross over the fine line where we may be lumped in with the fanatics. We don't want others to think Jesus defines who we are, because the world might judge us and it starts to feel like following Christ comes at too high a price.

While we struggle with our faith and our commitment to Jesus Christ, along comes the world, full of endless opportunities for selfish pleasure and indulgence. Just as Demas loved the age in which he lived, so we love the world around us. We do. *I* do. What's not to love? We have cool machines that give you money if you put your card in them. We have these little devices where, apparently a woman lives inside, who tells us how to get where we're going. We can record our favorite television shows and watch them whenever we want. We have computers which allow us to speak with people halfway around the world in real-time. We get pizza delivered in less than 30 minutes and our dry cleaning done in less than a day. We even have shampoo and conditioner in one bottle. What's not to love about our world?

In all seriousness, the fact that our world offers so much and demands so little causes us to believe that more will ultimately be enough. We falsely believe that if we acquire just a little bit more, someday soon we will be satisfied; that our deep thirst will be quenched. It is that illusion that continues to lead us away from our faith, from the one thing in our life that should be the source of our singular, undeniable purpose. It is the lie that if we just had a little bit more—a better job, a sleeker car, a new relationship, a longer vacation, a bigger house, a trimmer body—then we would be satisfied. Such thoughts are insidious, but I hope you are wise enough to know—at least on some level—that more will *never* be enough.

I have the privilege of being in a small group with some men I dearly love. Each one has a deep and abiding love for the Lord, and each one has achieved a level of success in business that is pretty rare. Through their gifts and skills, they have created businesses that bless their families while also employing many others. If you looked at any of them from the outside, you would say, "There goes a very successful man." One day not long ago, we met for about two hours. I'm not sure how the conversation started, but it came around to our current levels of stress and the burdens we feel on a daily basis. According to the world, these men had achieved everything one needs to be happy, and yet they had reached a place where they were acutely aware that none of those things mattered. What mattered was finding a way to live out God's call to be a true disciple, to care for and lead one's family. That was it. They knew it. We all knew it, but I am amazed at how many people just won't believe it. It's a lesson that often has to be learned the hard way.

In choosing to forsake Paul and his fellow workers, Demas forgot that nothing in the world lasts. The game ends. Eventually, it all goes away. If we all wind up with are things, but no meaning, then life is profoundly empty. None of what we achieve or earn is lasting. None of what the world gives us is lasting. A businessman playing tennis has a sudden sharp pain in his chest and within hours, his life is over. A family returning home from a movie collides head-on with a drunken driver and instantly it's over. A routine visit to the doctor's office reveals that the pain in your side is more than you thought it was and suddenly, all your priorities change. The cars, houses, clothes, trips, clubs, degrees, portfolios, collections—it all ends. None of it is eternal, and therefore, none of it holds any value for us or for those we love.

The One Thing That Matters

So then, what *is* of value? We find it back where Demas started. We find it rooted in a mission given to us by God, to be the ambassadors of His truth and the builders of His Kingdom. We are the "fellow workers" of Paul and John, Martin Luther and John Calvin, Billy Graham and Chuck Colson and so many others; the "fellow workers" of every single person committed to seeing lives transformed by the healing touch of Jesus Christ. The things that are important in life are clearly revealed when we come face to face with the reality that everything the world offers ultimately fails. It all ends.

Paul actually had it figured out in Philippians 3:8 when he said:

> *"I consider everything a loss compared to the surpassing greatness of knowing Christ Jesus, my Lord, for whose sake I have lost all things. I consider them rubbish that I may gain Christ and be found in Him..."*

The world and all it offers is rubbish—garbage—compared with the surpassing greatness of knowing Christ Jesus as Lord. Is it the simple way or the easy way? No. Does it require something of us? Yes. However, in light of what God has given us at the cross, the light of eternal life and the forgiveness of our sins—not to mention the chance to share that truth and see lives transformed in powerful and miraculous ways—it is a gift worth sacrificing for.

Twenty years from today, I wonder where I'll be. I have no idea if I will still be living in the same place or working in the same position, but I do know this: I hope and pray that I will still maintain a faithful, healthy relationship with God. I pray that I will not be trapped or enticed by our world, but rather living with the sure and certain hope that nothing compares to the surpassing greatness of knowing Christ. I pray that you will be following Christ; that you will be living in community, seeking God in every aspect of your life and living with the clear conviction of what is truly important. I pray that you will not only profess your faith in Jesus Christ, but actually live out of the abundance He promised us as His disciples.

If you've never made such a commitment, perhaps now is the time to say, "I am tired of the world and I see its emptiness. I see that nothing in this life lasts. I want to come home to my Father and to His Son who died for me. I want a life and a purpose that has ultimate and eternal value." Perhaps this is the time when you realize that you have more in common with Demas than you might like to admit. You haven't necessarily forsaken your faith or renounced Christ, but maybe you've gotten sidetracked from the mission and purpose Christ intended for your life—the wonder of a love relationship with God in Christ. Perhaps now is the time for you to come home, to return to your fellow workers and rejoin in the building of God's Kingdom on earth, to say, "I want to build kingdoms for God's Heaven and not kingdoms of this world."

Come Home

I'm not sure where I first heard this story or even if it is completely true. At one time, I was told that Ernest Hemingway had written about it. But regardless, the point of the story is true:

"No one could really say why he ran away. Or perhaps he didn't, but was kicked out of his home by his father for something foolish that he said or did. Either way, Paco found himself wandering the streets of Madrid, Spain with hopes of entering into a profession that would most likely get him killed—bullfighting.

Those who train under a mentor have a good chance of surviving this profession, but Paco's memory of his mistakes and guilt over what happened blindly drove him towards self-destruction. No doubt, that was the last thing his father wanted. Desperate to get his son back, he tried something that he hoped and prayed might work. Finding his son by wandering the streets of Madrid would be like finding a needle in a haystack, so Paco's father put an ad in the local newspaper, El Liberal. The advertisement read, 'Paco, meet me at the Hotel Montana at noon on Tuesday. All is forgiven! Love, Papa.'

Paco is such a common name in Spain that when the father went to the Hotel Montana the next day at noon, he found an amazing sight. He found not one young man, but more than 800 young men named Paco waiting for their fathers...and waiting for the forgiveness they never thought was possible!"

Jesus said in John 10:10, "I came that you might have life and have it to the fullest." Jesus came that we might have a rich, abundant life. Even so, many of us do not experience that abundance. We find it, and we avoid Demas' fate, when we remember the simple truth that the world and all it offers is but a temporary, fleeting satisfaction. The one, eternal, lasting gift of God is the gift of salvation we receive through His son, Jesus Christ. Whatever difficulty you may face, whatever persecution or hardship or sacrifice, is nothing compared to what Christ has given. It is my prayer that we experience conviction of purpose, clarity of focus, and an unwavering commitment in the face of a world of choices that would lead us to believe otherwise. God, in and through the power of His Holy Spirit, will give us the courage and wisdom we need to live a vital, healthy life in Christ.

For more information about Dr. Swanson and his ministry, go to these websites:

First Presbyterian Church, Orlando
www.fpco.org

The Well
www.drinkfromthewell.com

Conversant Media Group

Conversant Media Group is the creative force behind *Conversantlife.com*, a content rich new-media website that encourages conversations about faith and culture through expert blogs, social news, video, podcasts, and community participation.

Conversant Media Group utilizes a "collaborative publishing" business model and digital print technologies to produce engaging books offered in traditional print as well as various electronic formats.

www.ConversantMediaGroup.com

www.ConversantLife.com

LaVergne, TN USA
27 April 2010
180712LV00002B/2/P